THE KITCHEN CUPBOARD CHEF

THE KITCHEN CUPBOARD CHEF

Inspired recipes using canned, jarred & bottled ingredients

THEO A. MICHAELS
PHOTOGRAPHY BY MOWIE KAY

RYLAND PETERS & SMALL

Dedicated to my beautiful wife Anna and our kids,
Eva, Lex and Luca x

ART DIRECTOR Leslie Harrington
EDITORIAL DIRECTOR Julia Charles
SENIOR EDITOR Gillian Haslam
PRODUCTION MANAGER
Gordana Simakovic
PUBLISHER Cindy Richards

FOOD STYLIST Kathy Kordalis
PROP STYLIST Polly Webb-Wilson
INDEXER Hilary Bird

Originally published as *Canned* in 2021.
This edition published in 2026 by
Ryland Peters & Small
20–21 Jockey's Fields
London WC1R 4BW
and
1452 Davis Bugg Road,
Warrenton, NC 27589
www.rylandpeters.com
email: euregulations@rylandpeters.com

ISBN: 978-1-78879-713-9

10 9 8 7 6 5 4 3 2 1

Printed and bound in China.

CIP data from the Library of Congress has been applied for. A CIP record for this book is available from the British Library.

The authorised representative in the EEA is Authorised Rep Compliance Ltd., Ground Floor, 71 Lower Baggot Street, Dublin, D02 P593, Ireland
www.arccompliance.com

NOTES

- Both British (metric) and American (imperial plus US cups) measurements are included in these recipes; however, it is important to work with one set of measurements and not alternate between the two within a recipe.
- All butter is salted unless specified.
- All eggs are medium (UK) or large (US), unless specified as large, in which case US extra-large should be used. Uncooked or partially cooked eggs should not be served to the very old, frail, young children, pregnant women or those with compromised immune systems.
- Ovens should be preheated to the specified temperatures. We recommend using an oven thermometer. If using a fan-assisted oven, adjust temperatures according to the manufacturer's instructions.
- When a recipe calls for the grated zest of citrus fruit, buy unwaxed fruit and wash well before using. If you can only find treated fruit, scrub well in warm soapy water before using.
- Olive oil: extra-virgin olive oil is the highest quality oil. It is unrefined, contains antioxidants and anti-inflammatories and has a low smoke point and heightened flavour. It is best saved for dressings. Refined olive oil is milder in flavour and contains less health benefits but its higher smoke point makes it more suitable for cooking.

MIX
Paper | Supporting responsible forestry
FSC® C106563

CONTENTS

RED
450g
APOLLO
SARDINAS EN ACEITE VEGETAL
PESO NETO : 125g - PESO ESCURRIDO : 90g
SARDINES
in soya oil /in sojaolie/in Sojaöl
BRUNSWICK

INTRODUCTION

The following pages feature a collection of over 65 deliciously clever (though I say so myself) recipes that make canned ingredients the star of the show. Developing recipes for any cookbook always involves plenty of trial and error – long hours spent testing ingredients, experimenting with flavours and textures, and trying out new techniques (and on this occasion, wearing out several can openers!).

Finding my perfect 'cast' of cans to work with for these recipes took a fair amount of auditioning. There were, of course, the instant leads that appealed to my Mediterranean roots (delicate sardine fillets in golden olive oil were straight in), closely followed by the established supporting acts that have long had a role in my kitchen productions (i.e. chopped tomatoes and cooked beans). But I also discovered a few newcomers whose potential took me by surprise and have since become firm favourites in our household. There were of course, regretably, some that didn't make the cut, so you won't find them on these pages.

So why canned food? Canning food was born out of necessity, as a means of preserving food safely and to ensure, not only a supply out of season, but food that could be transported long distances, initally to troops on the front line during the Napoleonic wars. And of course canned produce also lasts forever. Well okay, almost... In 1974, samples were taken from cans found on a steamboat which sank nearly 100 years earlier, and found to be completely food safe. Of course, you wouldn't want to eat it. It looked horrible, smelled worse and was void of any nutritional content. But it was edible!

Decades in development, canned food was intially expensive to buy and out of the reach of us ordinary folk, and in more recent times it has become a polarizing subject. For a good number of people it conjures up images of rationing, austerity and 'making do' with poor substitutes for more expensive fresh foods. For others, it's filled with nostalgia and some brands enjoy an almost cult-like adoration worldwide – here's looking at you Spam! While in Europe, Spain and Italy in particular, canning is a highly acceptable way of preserving gourmet ingredients, from cured fish to ripe tomatoes, bursting with flavour that's captured at its peak and preferable to their fresh counterpart in some dishes.

Whatever your take, canned food is enjoying a comeback so it's time to look again. For my money, it is super convenient to have canned food within easy reach, added to which some cans offer shortcuts that reduce cooking times dramatically. It also provides us with the opportunity to discover interesting ingredients from all over the world (from okra to banana blossoms), and, as I have now learnt, can bring a different texture and flavour to what we've come to expect from our fresh food, allowing us (with a little ingenuity) to use them in new and different ways. As with my previous books, I celebrate the versatility of ingredients and have created recipes for you to cook, share, enjoy and tailor to suit your own tastes and needs. I hope you will find them all delicious, discover some new favourites, and be inspired to experiment to get the very most of your own stash of cans at home.

CANNED KNOW-HOW

STORE CUPBOARD ITEMS

Canned ingredients play an important part in my family's food and we always keep a wide selection on standby. You'll usually find the following in my store cupboard:

Beans, pulses/legumes and lentils

I use virtually every type of these regularly in cooking and the difference between using dried or canned is minimal, especially when they are part of a larger dish. The canned versions are also so much easier to use – simply open the can, drain, rinse and use (no need for overnight soaking and boiling). Baked beans in tomato sauce are also a great standby for a quick meal.

Tomatoes

Where would we be without good-quality canned tomatoes? Cherry tomatoes, passata/ sieved/strained tomatoes, chopped tomatoes – these make the base for so many recipes and I couldn't imagine not having cans of them lined up in the store cupboard!

Vegetables

I keep a good range of canned vegetables, such as sweetcorn/corn kernels, olives, spinach, water chestnuts, broad/fava beans, artichoke hearts, etc. Some vegetables from a can are just as good as fresh (sweetcorn/corn kernels, for example), while others like spinach have a totally different texture to fresh and I prefer to use the canned version in certain dishes, such as my Chana Saag Paneer on page 102. Some fresh vegetables, such as beansprouts, just don't keep for very long and always teeter on the edge of becoming food waste, so the canned versions are more convenient as a handy addition to a rustled-up meal. I also like to have a stock of chipotle peppers (in adobo sauce) and roasted red (bell) peppers, plus cans of ratatouille.

Fruit

I keep a stock of peaches, cherries, apricots and more (albeit I tend to stay away from the weird fruit salad concoction). Perfect for making a quick fruit crumble (see page 145) or for elevating into a fancier dish, such as the Balsamic Cherry Tarte Tatin on page 150.

Soups

Besides being a great standby meal, using soups as ready-made sauces makes for a great and delicious quick cheat (see my Creamy Tomato & Tuna Pasta Bake on page 84).

Fish and seafood

While some canned foods are a convenient substitute for using fresh, others, like good-quality canned fish/seafood are a delicacy in their own right. Anchovies, mackerel, tuna, sardines, smoked mussels, squid, etc. are all good and need no more than a slice of toast and a squeeze of lemon juice (and a glass of good wine) for a perfect lite bite. Equally, many are an integral ingredient to a broad range recipes.

Meat

Corned beef, good pork luncheon meat (I always use Spam) and chicken breast are always handy to have on standby as they have such a long shelf life. Canned French cassoulet is another ingredient that is useful as the base of a meal.

Milk products

I keep a stash of cans of coconut milk (useful for both sweet and savoury dishes), condensed milk and rice pudding (see the arancini on page 149).

Jars

I know I talk about 'cans' in all the recipes, but some store cupboard items tend to only be found in jars, like sundried/sunblush tomatoes, capers, olives, pickled eggs, etc. I've also found that certain brands of pulses/legumes in jars tend to be of a higher quality, so I always buy jars of chickpeas and butter beans when I spot them, as well as having cans of the same.

SUBSTITUTIONS

You can substitute canned ingredients in most of my recipes; in fact, I absolutely encourage you to do so! All of my cookbooks are written for you – so if you don't like a particular ingredient or don't have it to hand, swap it for something else! Swapping like for like – for example, one type of bean for another or a lentil, or swapping whole cherry tomatoes for passata/strained tomatoes or peaches for apricots – will often not affect the recipe much and if it means you enjoy the finished result more, then I say go for it!

Can sizes do vary from country to country, and from brand to brand, and unlike baking where measurements tend to be quite precise, most of my recipes won't be affected by a little more of this or a little less of that.

LEFTOVERS

For the most part, if I only use part of a canned item, I usually decant the leftovers into a non-reactive bowl, store it in the fridge and try to use the leftovers in a different recipe within the next day or two.

WHAT TO BUY

Some canned products come in a variety of liquids, such as oil, water, brine, etc. I tend to lean towards olive oil-based products as I've found that some of the ones stored in water have lost a little of their flavour.

Finally, not all canned products are created equal, so I encourage you to buy the best you can afford. This is especially true for ingredients you can serve straight from the can (for example, anchovies), so it's worth spending a little extra if you are able to.

SMALL BITES & SHARERS

ROASTED RED PEPPER & CHICKPEA HUMMUS

This delightfully quick and easy hummus is perfect as it comes, but is even better with a bit of tangy feta cheese crumbled over the top.

50 g/2 oz. roasted red (bell) peppers from a jar or can
400-g/14-oz. can chickpeas, drained (reserve a splash of the liquid)
3 tablespoons extra virgin olive oil
1 garlic clove, lightly crushed
2 teaspoons freshly squeezed lemon juice
½ fresh red chilli/chile (optional)
½ teaspoon salt
a little crumbled feta cheese (optional)

Makes about 500 g/2 cups

Add all the ingredients to a food processor (including a splash of chickpea liquid) and blitz until you have a smooth paste. Taste for seasoning, adding more lemon juice if preferred. Transfer to a serving bowl. If you wish, sprinkle a little crumbled feta over the top.

Feel free to add any soft green herbs you like to the food processor as another option (fresh basil works very well with the red pepper).

BROAD BEAN 'GUACAMOLE'

This dip wasn't meant to be a guacamole recipe! It started life as something entirely different, but the blended beans instantly reminded me of smashed avocado. So if you're experiencing an avocado shortage, try my totally inauthentic guacamole instead. This is good slathered on toast, topped with a poached egg and a drizzle of hot sauce (see photograph on page 2).

400-g/14-oz. can broad/fava beans (green), drained
½ garlic clove, crushed
60 ml/¼ cup extra virgin olive oil
½ teaspoon salt
1 teaspoon freshly squeezed lime juice
½ teaspoon malt vinegar
a pinch of ground cumin
1 spring onion/scallion, finely sliced
a few sprigs of fresh coriander/cilantro, chopped

Makes about 300 g/1¼ cups

Add all the ingredients except the spring onion/scallion and coriander/cilantro to a food processor. Pulse at first, then increase the speed until you have a coarsely puréed consistency. Fold in the spring onion/scallion and coriander/cilantro and taste, adding more salt, lime juice or cumin as preferred. Transfer to a serving bowl.

LEX'S TARAMASALATA

I've named this recipe after my son, Lex, as he and I are the only two out of our family of five who can devour an entire baguette with nothing more than a tub of this stuff to keep it company! He was my chief taster when I was developing this recipe.

200-g/7-oz. can cod roe, drained
1 small red onion, grated (about 20 g/2 tablespoons)
½ teaspoon cayenne pepper
2 tablespoons freshly squeezed lemon juice
1 chunky slice of toasted bread (about 50 g/2 oz.)
50 ml/3½ tablespoons milk
100 ml/7 tablespoons extra virgin olive oil, plus extra to serve
salt and freshly ground black pepper

TO SERVE
olives
toasted pitta bread

Makes about 500 g/2 cups

Add the drained cod roe to a food processor, breaking it up with the back of a fork, then add the grated onion, cayenne pepper and lemon juice and season generously with salt and freshly ground black pepper.

Soak the toasted bread in the milk for a minute, then squeeze out the excess liquid and tear the toast into the food processor (discard the leftover milk). Pulse everything in the food processor to begin with, then increase the speed and start drizzling in the olive oil until it has all been added.

Depending on consistency, I usually add a couple of tablespoons of water at the end to smooth the taramasalata. Taste, adding more salt, lemon juice or cayenne as preferred.

Serve in a bowl with a little extra drizzle of olive oil, traditionally with a few olives alongside and some toasted pitta bread for dipping.

SPICY HARISSA FALAFEL

Freshly made falafel are delicious and something I strongly recommend you try making at home. These ones are laced with Moroccan harissa paste, which gives a delicious hint of warming spice, complemented here by the cooling Greek yogurt.

2 x 400-g/14-oz. cans chickpeas, drained
1 small white onion, chopped
2 garlic cloves, chopped
1 tablespoon ground cumin, plus a pinch to garnish
1½ tablespoons coriander seeds, lightly crushed
a small bunch of fresh flat-leaf parsley (stalks and leaves)
a small bunch of fresh coriander/ cilantro (stalks and leaves), plus a few sprigs to garnish
1 teaspoon baking powder
1 teaspoon salt
65 g/½ cup plain/all-purpose flour
30 ml/2 tablespoons harissa paste, plus 1 teaspoon to garnish
vegetable oil, for deep-frying

TO SERVE
250 g/1 cup Greek yogurt
a pinch of nigella seeds

Serves 4

Place half the chickpeas and all the onion, garlic, cumin, coriander seeds, fresh parsley and coriander/ cilantro, baking powder, salt, flour and harissa paste in a food processor. Blend until just fully incorporated (be careful not to over-blend to a purée). Once fully incorporated, add the remaining chickpeas and pulse until broken down but still quite coarse (this gives your falafel texture).

Roll the mixture into falafel the size of ping-pong balls, then flatten slightly with the palm of your hand.

Heat the oil in a large saucepan; test whether it is hot enough by dropping a pinch of breadcrumbs into it – they should sizzle immediately but take at least 30 seconds before they turn golden. Deep-fry the falafel in the hot oil for 2–4 minutes until the exterior is crisp (you might need to do this in batches). Remove the cooked falafel using a slotted spoon and leave to drain on paper towels.

Pour the Greek yogurt onto a large serving dish and swirl a couple of ribbons of harissa paste through the yogurt to create beautiful swirls. Pile the falafel over one side of the yogurt, then dust with a pinch of cumin, nigella seeds and a few torn sprigs of coriander/cilantro.

ANTIPASTI SHARING BOARD

Having a stash of good-quality canned food to hand makes it easy to rustle up an Italian-style sharing board for an impromptu gathering. Buy the best quality products you can afford; there's no cooking hocus pocus here, so it's all about letting the ingredients shine. Plenty of the other recipes in this book would work well on sharers too – try Crispy Cockles (see page 21), Crab Fritters (see page 25), all the dips (see pages 13–14) and the Proper Pickled Scotch Eggs (see page 29).

1 baguette, cut into 1-cm/½-inch slices
olive oil
2 garlic cloves, halved
2 ripe vine tomatoes, sliced
50-g/2-oz. can anchovies (I like Cantabrian ones), drained
a few fresh basil leaves
100-g/3½-oz. can boneless sardines in olive oil, drained
freshly grated zest and juice of 1 lemon
150-g/5½-oz. can pitted/stoned black olives, drained
400-g/14-oz. can palm hearts, drained and sliced into discs
a few pinches of chilli/hot red pepper flakes
a few sprigs of fresh flat-leaf parsley, finely chopped
salt and freshly ground black pepper

Serves about 6 as a sharer

Baguette toasts: drizzle a little olive oil over the baguette slices on both sides, toast under a preheated grill/broiler for a couple of minutes, then season lightly.

Tomato and anchovy: rub the cut side of a garlic clove over the baguette toasts, top with tomato slices, a drizzle of olive oil and a couple of anchovies, finish with a basil leaf and freshly ground black pepper.

Citrus sardines: pile a few sardines on the baguette toasts, finish with a squeeze of lemon and a pinch of freshly ground black pepper; nothing more is needed.

Tapenade: place most of the drained olives (reserve a few to garnish the board) into a food processor with 30 ml/2 tablespoons olive oil, half a crushed garlic clove and a generous pinch of salt. Pulse to a semi-coarse paste. Taste and add more garlic or salt if needed and finish with a squeeze of lemon. Spread on the baguette toasts and add a drizzle of olive oil or transfer to a bowl and serve as a dip.

Garlic palm hearts: crush half a garlic clove and whisk into 30 ml/2 tablespoons olive oil with a pinch each of salt, chilli/hot red pepper flakes and finely chopped parsley, plus the zest of half a lemon. Fold the palm hearts through the dressing.

Garnish: I like to include the following on my sharing board: smoked squid or octopus pieces, artichoke hearts, caper berries, olives, roasted red peppers, sun-blushed tomatoes, rocket/arugula, grapes, cheeses, chutneys and extra bread.

CRISPY COCKLES

These deep-fried, crispy cockles dusted with cayenne pepper make a delicious anytime nibble. Serve them with a creamy mustard mayo on the side and wash down with an ice-cold beer.

2 x 120-g/4½-oz. cans cockles, drained
60 g/½ cup plain/all-purpose flour
60 g/½ cup cornflour/cornstarch
1 teaspoon cayenne pepper
salt and freshly ground black pepper
vegetable oil, for frying

MUSTARD MAYO
125 ml/½ cup mayonnaise
1 tablespoon English mustard

Serves 4 as a snack

Mustard mayo: mix the mayonnaise and mustard together and set aside.

Place the drained cockles between two sheets of paper towels and gently push down to absorb as much moisture as possible. You may need to replace the paper towels once or twice.

In a clean bowl, mix together the two flours and the cayenne pepper, then season with salt and freshly ground black pepper. Add the cockles to the bowl, turning them over with a spoon to fully coat them in the flour mixture.

Pour the vegetable oil into a frying pan/skillet to a depth of about 1 cm/½ inch and heat. When hot, shake the excess flour from the cockles and drop one of them into the pan. If the oil is too hot it will pop and spit; if that happens, turn the heat down a fraction. Add the remaining cockles and fry for about 3–4 minutes until really crispy. Use a slotted spoon to remove the cockles and drain on paper towels. Season with salt immediately.

Serve with the mustard mayo on the side.

CRAB & BEER FONDUE IN A BREAD BOWL

Fondue is perhaps the ultimate sharer. This store-cupboard rustle-up is a cheat's recipe rather than an authentic fondue, but I think it tastes just as good. The beer not only gives it a rich flavour, but also helps aerate the fondue mixture, giving it a lighter texture. I think the beer and Cheddar make a great pairing here, but feel free to play around with other cheeses and sparkling booze (such as cider, Prosecco, etc).

400-g/14-oz. rustic cob loaf
olive oil
35 g/2½ tablespoons butter
35 g/¼ cup plain/all-purpose flour
300 ml/1¼ cups milk
100 g/1 cup Cheddar cheese, grated/shredded
2 x 145-g/5¼-oz. cans lump crab meat, drained
125 ml/½ cup beer (I like to use lager or Pilsner)
a pinch of paprika
a few sprigs of fresh flat-leaf parsley or celery leaves, finely chopped
celery sticks/stalks, to serve
salt and freshly ground black pepper

Serves 4

Preheat the oven to 200°C fan/220°C/425°F/Gas 7.

First, prepare the bread bowl. Carefully slice about 5 cm/2 inches off the top of the loaf and scoop out the bread with your fingers to create a bowl-shaped hollow. Lightly oil the inside of the loaf, massaging the oil over the bread. Tear the scooped-out bread into 5-cm/2-inch pieces. Place everything (the bread bowl and the bread pieces) onto a baking sheet and pop into the preheated oven for 10 minutes.

Meanwhile, make a béchamel sauce – melt the butter in a saucepan, add the flour and cook for a couple of minutes, stirring constantly, over a gentle heat. Remove the pan from the heat, slowly whisk in the milk little by little and season generously with salt and freshly ground black pepper. Return the pan to the heat and keep stirring until it starts to bubble, then whisk in the cheese, remove from the heat and fold in the crab meat.

Pour the beer into the sauce, gently stir it through and pour the whole lot into the bread bowl. Sprinkle with a small pinch of paprika and the chopped celery leaves or parsley. Serve immediately with the oven-baked bread pieces and sticks/stalks of celery (or any other crudités of your choice) – you may need to pierce them onto forks for dipping.

SOUTHERN-STYLE CRAB FRITTERS
WITH RÉMOULADE SAUCE

These Deep South-style crab fritters are perfect for sharing. Just make sure you make enough of the spicy rémoulade sauce to go around!

2 x 145-g/5¼-oz. cans lump crab meat
1 tablespoons capers, coarsely chopped
a few sprigs of fresh dill and flat-leaf parsley, chopped
1 teaspoon Worcestershire sauce
a pinch of salt
1 egg
150 g/3 cups fresh breadcrumbs
vegetable oil, for shallow frying

SPICY RÉMOULADE SAUCE

250 ml/1 cup mayonnaise
1 tablespoon Dijon mustard
1 tablespoon tomato ketchup
1 garlic clove, crushed
1 tablespoon paprika
1 teaspoon hot sauce, such as Tabasco
2 tablespoons capers, coarsely chopped
a small squeeze of fresh lemon juice
¼ teaspoon salt

Makes 12

Start by making the spicy rémoulade sauce; mix all the ingredients together and taste, adding a little more of any of the ingredients to your taste. Set aside.

To make the fritters, place the crab meat in a sieve/strainer and gently push down to extract the excess liquid, then leave to drain.

Place the capers, herbs, Worcestershire sauce, salt and egg in a mixing bowl, add 4 tablespoons of the spicy rémoulade sauce and whisk together, ensuring the egg is all fully incorporated. Fold in one-third of the breadcrumbs and all the crab meat, trying not to over-mix.

Place the remaining breadcrumbs in a flat dish. Take a ping-pong ball-sized portion of the crab mixture, roll into a ball between the palms of your hands and then flatten a little (the mixture will be slightly wet which is perfect for coating in the remaining breadcrumbs). Roll the ball in the breadcrumbs, coating it on all sides. Repeat with the remaining mixture to make 12 fritters.

Heat enough vegetable oil to coat the bottom of a saucepan. Fry the fritters for 2–4 minutes on each side until golden (you may need to cook them in batches to avoid over-crowding the pan). Remove from the pan and set on paper towels to drain. Season with a pinch of salt and transfer to a serving dish with the remaining spicy rémoulade on the side.

CRAB ROLLS

We really enjoyed eating fresh crab and lobster on a regular basis during the time we lived in New Jersey, especially when we travelled up the coast. These tasty and tangy treats are my store-cupboard interpretation of New England's classic crab rolls, for when wrestling a live crab into a pot isn't an available option...

2 x 145-g/5¼-oz. cans lump crab meat
4 ciabatta rolls, or similar
1 Little Gem lettuce/baby Cos or Romaine, shredded (optional)

DRESSING

45 ml/3 tablespoons mayonnaise
a sprig of fresh dill, chopped (or 1 teaspoon dried dill)
1 tablespoon diced red onion
a few drops of freshly squeezed lemon juice
a pinch of cayenne pepper
½ teaspoon Worcestershire sauce
a pinch of salt and freshly ground black pepper

Serves 4

In a bowl, whisk together all the dressing ingredients until fully incorporated. Season to taste. Drain the crab meat and gently fold into the dressing, being careful not to break up the meat too much.

Slice the ciabatta rolls in half and toast the cut sides. Line the base of the rolls with some shredded lettuce, if using, and spoon on the crab filling. Top with more lettuce, if using, and add the tops of the rolls to serve.

PROPER PICKLED SCOTCH EGGS

This ingenious recipe (if I do say so myself...) takes store-bought pickled eggs, wraps them in haggis then breadcrumbs and deep-fries them until crispy. The sharpness of the pickled egg helps cut through the richness of the haggis. Slice them open and serve with a little onion chutney or English mustard, whatever you prefer. Perfect for lunch with a salad or just enjoy them as a bar snack.

1 egg
150 g/1 cup plus 2 tablespoons plain/all-purpose flour
120 g/generous 2 cups fresh breadcrumbs
4 pickled eggs (from a jar)
395-g/14-oz. can haggis
vegetable oil, for deep frying
onion chutney, English mustard or tangy relish of your choice, to serve

Makes 4

Whisk the egg in a bowl with a splash of water to make an egg wash. Place the flour in a second bowl and the breadcrumbs in a third. Rinse the pickled eggs, pat dry and place in the bowl with the flour.

Take a quarter of the haggis from the can and flatten with the back of a fork to a thickness of about 5 mm/¼ inch or less. Lift this into the palm of your hand (it will break and that's fine). With the other hand, roll one of the pickled eggs in the flour, shake off the excess and place the floured pickled egg in the middle of the flattened haggis in your hand. Now mould the haggis around the egg, adding more bits of haggis until it is fully encased. Once you've got a nice tight ball, roll the haggis-covered egg in the flour. Shake off the excess, then dip into the egg wash, turning to fully coat it, then roll in the breadcrumbs to coat, patting them down. Repeat until all four Scotch eggs are made.

Pour the vegetable oil into a saucepan to a depth of about 5 cm/2 inches and heat. Test the temperature by dropping a piece of haggis into the oil – it should sizzle immediately but take 30 seconds before it starts floating.

When you're ready, carefully lower the Scotch eggs into the hot oil (do this in batches); fry for a couple of minutes on each side until golden and crisp. Remove using a slotted spoon and place on paper towels to drain. Cut in half and serve with your choice of chutney, mustard or relish.

Organic
Chickpeas
monJardin

SOUPS & SALADS

RICH ONION SOUP
WITH CHEESE TOASTS

A French onion soup is delicious, but we all know it's a labour of love to make – slicing all those onions and slowly cooking for ages until caramelized and golden. Using canned onions I've created a fast-track recipe that produces something tasty but cooked in only 30 minutes. And of course the cheese toast floating on the top is a must!

30 g/2 tablespoons butter
1 tablespoon olive oil
425-g/15-oz. can sautéed onions
3 garlic cloves, chopped
1 bay leaf
1 teaspoon brown sugar
2 tablespoons plain/all-purpose flour
45 ml/3 tablespoons brandy
1 litre/4 cups beef-chicken stock, made with 2 stock cubes (1 beef and 1 chicken)
1 teaspoon balsamic vinegar
1 baguette
100 g/1 scant cup grated/shredded Gruyère cheese or similar
salt and freshly ground black pepper

Serves 4

Melt the butter with the olive oil in a heavy-based, high-sided frying pan/skillet. Add the canned onions, garlic and bay leaf and season with salt and freshly ground black pepper. Sweat the onions for about 10 minutes over a medium/high heat, stirring frequently, then add the sugar and cook for another 5 minutes until the onions turn a dark golden hue.

Stir in the flour, cook for a further minute, then whisk in the brandy and a ladleful of the stock and boil for a minute to burn off the alcohol. Stir in the balsamic vinegar and remaining stock, bring to a simmer, then reduce to a very gentle heat while you prepare the cheese toasts.

Slice the baguette into eight thin slices, toast on both sides and then sprinkle the grated/shredded cheese over the top whilst they are still hot. Leave to cool slightly while you ladle the soup into serving bowls. Place two melting cheese toasts in each bowl of soup, add a few grinds of black pepper and serve. (You can pop the bowls under a preheated grill/ broiler to further melt the cheese, if you wish.)

ANNA'S PEA, HAM & BORLOTTI BEAN SOUP

My wife Anna doesn't like peas – it's the one thing I've not managed to convert her to over the years, unlike buying a puppy, staying in a youth hostel and getting curtains for the kitchen (I lied, the curtains are under negotiation), so you can imagine my surprise when I saw her devouring a bowl of this pea and ham soup. Thus this soup shall always be known as Anna's pea soup! It's a deliciously hearty soup and you can happily swap the borlotti/cranberry beans for canned lentils or any other pulse/legume.

a splash of olive oil
2 garlic cloves, chopped
200-g/7-oz. can lean ham, diced into 1-cm/½-inch cubes
2 x 300-g/10½-oz. cans garden peas
400-g/14-oz. can borlotti/cranberry beans, drained and rinsed
250 ml/1 cup chicken stock, made with ½ stock cube
a small knob/pat of butter
a pinch of paprika (optional)
salt and freshly ground black pepper

Serves 4

Heat a small splash of olive oil in a large saucepan, add the garlic and three-quarters of the diced ham and fry for a couple of minutes, then pour in both cans of peas including their liquid and add two-thirds of the drained borlotti/cranberry beans. Bring to a gentle simmer and cook for about a minute, then mash as much as possible using a potato masher. Season generously with freshly ground black pepper and a pinch of salt.

Pour in the chicken stock and the remaining beans (reserve a few to garnish if you wish) and bring to a simmer, stirring frequently for a minute or two, then remove from the heat.

Once the soup has stopped bubbling, stir in the butter and pour into serving bowls. Top each one with the remaining ham and beans, then add a little swirl of olive oil and a small pinch of paprika (if using).

MACKEREL MARMITAKO

Marmitako is a humble fish stew from the Basque region of Spain, named after the pot it's cooked in, the marmita. It is traditionally made with tuna and I've taken inspiration from it for my canned version, but I've chosen to use smoky mackerel fillets in their own tomato sauce.

1 onion, diced
a splash of olive oil
1 garlic clove, chopped
225-g/8-oz. can piquillo peppers, drained and roughly chopped
400-g/14-oz. can new potatoes, drained and cut into 2.5 cm/1-inch cubes
1 teaspoon smoked paprika
½ teaspoon salt
750 ml/3¼ cups chicken stock (made with 1 stock cube)
2 x 145-g/5¼-oz. cans mackerel fillets in spicy tomato sauce
a few sprigs of fresh flat-leaf parsley, roughly chopped
freshly ground black pepper

Serves 4

Fry the onion in a splash of olive oil in a large pan for 5 minutes until soft, then add the garlic and peppers and cook for a few more minutes.

Add the potatoes to the pan, along with the smoked paprika and salt. Mash a few chunks of potato with the back of a fork to help release some of their starch into the soup and leave to cook for a couple of minutes, then pour in the stock and simmer gently for a few minutes.

Add the mackerel to the pan along with all the sauce (I swill a spoonful of the soup around the cans to pick up any sauce left behind and pour it in). Immediately remove the pan from the heat. Taste, add more salt if needed and finish with chopped parsley and a grinding of black pepper.

CRAB LAKSA

I was first introduced to laksa while travelling in China many years ago. We had arrived at our hostel at 1 am, cold and hungry, and as if by magic steaming bowls of laksa were placed in front of us. We were so very grateful and it's something I'll never forget. This recipe is inspired by my memories of that first encounter with the dish, except it uses crab rather than chicken and canned vegetables... and is eaten in the comfort of my own home and at around 1 pm...

200 g/7 oz. vermicelli rice noodles
1 lemongrass stalk
2 tablespoons olive oil
1 tablespoon sesame oil
1 red onion, grated
2 garlic cloves, grated
5-cm/2-inch piece of fresh ginger, peeled and grated
1 fresh red chilli/chile, finely chopped
½ teaspoon ground turmeric
1 tablespoon tomato purée/paste
400-ml/14-oz. can coconut milk
1 tablespoon fish sauce
1 tablespoon smooth peanut butter
½ tablespoon brown sugar
225-g/8-oz. can sliced water chestnuts, drained
500 ml/2 cups chicken or vegetable stock (made with 1 stock cube)
400-g/14-oz. can cut green beans, drained
2 x 145-g/5¼-oz. cans lump crab meat, drained
a few sprigs of fresh coriander/cilantro, to garnish
1 lime, cut into wedges, to serve
salt

Serves 4

Place the noodles in a large mixing bowl, submerge in just-boiled water and leave to hydrate while you prepare the soup.

Bash the lemongrass, discard the outer leaf and finely chop. Add both the oils to a heavy-based frying pan/skillet over a medium heat. Once hot, stir in the onion, garlic, ginger, chilli/chile, lemongrass and turmeric and cook for a few minutes; be careful not to let the mixture burn.

Stir in the tomato purée/paste, followed by the coconut milk, continually stirring to ensure everything is incorporated, then add the fish sauce, peanut butter, sugar, water chestnuts and stock. Leave this to bubble away gently until you are ready to serve.

To serve, line up your serving bowls (if they are very cold, swill some boiling water around them to take the chill off as it will keep your soup warmer for longer).

Tip the green beans into the pan of soup. Drain the noodles and divide amongst the warmed serving bowls. Use a slotted spoon to scoop the green beans from the pan and add to the bowls first, grouping them together. Divide the drained crab meat amongst the bowls, again, grouping it together. Finally, ladle the hot soup into each bowl, sharing out the water chestnuts. Garnish with coriander/cilantro, lime wedges and a sprinkle of salt. If you have any chilli/chile leftover, you can scatter over a few pieces.

CHARRED CANNELLINI BEAN SALAD

I found out that charring the cannellini beans changes their texture and flavour slightly, and for the better. Rosemary adds an earthy note and it's all livened up with a tangy lemon and garlic dressing.

2 x 400-g/14-oz. cans cannellini beans, drained and rinsed
125 ml/½ cup extra virgin olive oil
a knob/pat of butter
leaves from 2 sprigs of fresh rosemary
1 small garlic clove, crushed
freshly squeezed juice of ½ lemon
a few sprigs of fresh flat-leaf parsley, chopped (optional)
salt and freshly ground black pepper

Serves 2 as a main; 4 as a side

Pat the drained and rinsed cannellini beans dry with paper towels (if you wish, do this the day before and leave in the fridge, uncovered – they need to be completely dry and this helps to achieve that).

Heat a heavy-based frying pan/skillet until almost smoking, then pour in half the olive oil and the butter. Once the butter has stopped foaming, carefully toss in the cannellini beans and give the pan a little shake to level them out; you may have to do this in batches if they don't fit in one layer.

Season generously with salt and freshly ground black pepper, scatter the rosemary over the top and do not move the beans. Just leave the beans over a high heat for 2 minutes, without moving or stirring them. Once you notice they are charring or after the 2 minutes are up, tip the beans onto a flat plate or baking sheet and leave to cool.

Whisk together the remaining olive oil, the garlic, lemon juice and chopped parsley (if using) and drizzle this dressing over the cooled cannellini beans just before serving.

BLACK-EYED BEAN & TUNA SALAD

This simple black-eyed bean/pea and tuna salad is the perfect solution when you want a little taste of the Mediterranean. Serve a generous helping with good bread, or as a side to a main meal.

2 x 400-g/14-oz. cans black-eyed beans/peas
1 small red onion, thinly sliced
about 80 g/3 oz. pitted/stoned black olives, drained and cut in half
a pinch of dried oregano
a small bunch each of fresh flat-leaf parsley and coriander/cilantro, roughly chopped
145-g/5¼-oz. can or jar of tuna, drained
75 ml/5 tablespoons extra virgin olive oil
freshly squeezed juice of 1 lemon
1 tablespoon white wine vinegar
salt and freshly ground black pepper

Serves 4 as a main; 8 as a side

Drain and rinse the beans/peas, shaking off any excess water. Add to a mixing bowl along with the sliced onion, olives, dried oregano and fresh herbs, season with salt and freshly ground black pepper and mix together. Once fully incorporated, gently fold in the tuna to avoid it breaking up too much.

Lightly whisk together the olive oil, lemon juice and vinegar, then pour this dressing over the salad and fold it through a couple of times before serving.

CORONATION SALMON
IN LETTUCE CUPS

This easy recipe is mighty tasty and salmon makes a nice change from the tuna mayonnaise we are all too familiar with. Serving it in lettuce 'cups' adds a nice summery crunch, but in winter months I prefer to eat it spread over some hot buttered toast. The heat will vary depending on your curry powder – I used medium-hot, but you could use mild or hot and just adjust it to suit your own tastes.

10 g/1 tablespoon raisins
250 ml/1 cup mayonnaise
1 scant tablespoon medium-hot curry powder
1 tablespoon orange and ginger marmalade/preserve (or regular marmalade)
½ small red onion, finely diced (about 1 tablespoon)
a few sprigs of fresh flat-leaf parsley, chopped
freshly squeezed juice of 1 lemon
2 x 200-g/7-oz. cans pink salmon
2 Cos/Romaine lettuce hearts (optional)
salt and freshly ground black pepper

Serves 4

Place the raisins in a heatproof bowl and pour over just enough boiled water to cover, then leave to plump up while you make the rest of the dish.

Mix together the mayonnaise, curry powder, marmalade/preserve, red onion and chopped parsley and season with a pinch of salt and freshly ground black pepper. Squeeze in a little lemon juice and taste for seasoning, adding more curry powder or marmalade as needed. Drain the raisins and fold them through.

Open both cans of salmon, drain and pick through, removing any bones and skin, or as much as possible. Fold the salmon into the dressing, letting it break up a little as you do.

Separate the lettuce hearts into leaves, allowing a couple of lettuce leaves per serving, and divide the salmon mixture amongst the leaves. Serve as soon as possible after assembling otherwise the leaves will go soggy.

GRIDDLED APRICOT & GRAIN SALAD

This mixed grain, nut and canned fruit salad is delicious served as a summery main course or side dish. It's flexible too, as you can swap out the pouch of pre-cooked mixed grains for Puy lentils or a couple of cans of drained chickpeas. If you want to increase the volume of the salad, just add a few handfuls of mixed baby salad leaves. I sometimes serve it with a dollop of Greek yogurt on the side too.

15 g/2 tablespoons sultanas/golden raisins
½ teaspoon cumin seeds
15 g/½ oz. mixed nuts
250-g/9-oz. pouch pre-cooked mixed grains (you can use any combination of wheatberries, rice, freekah, barley, quinoa, etc.)
410-g/14½-oz. can apricot halves in syrup
1 teaspoon runny honey
1 teaspoon sherry vinegar
1 tablespoon extra virgin olive oil
a few sprigs of fresh herbs, such as flat-leaf parsley, mint and/or coriander/cilantro, roughly chopped
salt and freshly ground black pepper
Greek yogurt, to serve (optional)

Serves 4

Place the sultanas/golden raisins in a bowl and pour over just enough boiled water to cover, then leave to plump up while you make the rest of the dish.

Add the mixed grains to a large mixing bowl. Toast the cumin seeds and nuts in a dry frying pan/skillet, then lightly crush and add to the bowl.

Drain the apricot halves, reserving 60 ml/ 4 tablespoons of the syrup. Cut the apricot halves in half again. Preheat a griddle pan and when smoking hot, place the apricot pieces in the pan for a couple of minutes on each side until charred. Add the charred apricots to the bowl with the grains.

Whisk together the reserved apricot syrup with the honey, vinegar, olive oil and a pinch of salt and freshly ground black pepper and pour this dressing over the salad.

Drain the sultanas and add to the salad, then fold in the chopped herbs. Mix everything together, then transfer to a clean serving dish and serve with a dollop of Greek yogurt on the side (if using).

BUDDHA BOWL

A buddha bowl should be a vegetarian dish, in keeping with the principles of buddhism, and full of delicious and tempting contrasts of flavour, colour and texture, which is what I've aimed to create here. You can make all the elements of this in advance, or prepare it and serve immediately.

400-g/14-oz. can chickpeas, drained and rinsed
1 tablespoon runny honey or maple syrup
1 tablespoon dark soy sauce
400-g/14-oz. can baby carrots
½ tablespoon sesame oil
a pinch of toasted sesame seeds
50 ml/3½ tablespoons sriracha sauce
100 ml/7 tablespoons mayonnaise, or vegan equivalent if preferred
2 x 400-g/14-oz. cans pearl barley
a handful of fresh mint leaves, chopped, plus a few extra sprigs to garnish
a handful of fresh coriander/cilantro, chopped, plus a few extra sprigs to garnish
1 pickled or peeled hard-boiled/cooked egg, grated (optional)
1 tablespoon olive oil
2 limes
400-g/14-oz. can mango slices in natural juice, drained and cut into 2.5-cm/1-inch cubes
½ fresh red chilli/chile, finely diced
4 flour tortillas (optional)
200-g/7-oz. can edamame beans, drained
salt and freshly ground black pepper

Serves 4

Preheat the oven to 200°C fan/220°C/425°F/Gas 7.

Honey and soy roasted chickpeas: Dry the chickpeas on paper towels, lay them out on a baking sheet and bake in the preheated oven for 15 minutes. Mix the honey or maple syrup and half the soy sauce together. Remove the chickpeas from the oven and pour the honey-soy mixture over them, ensuring they are well coated, then return to the oven for a further 7 minutes. Once done, shake them, season with a pinch of salt and tip onto a flat plate.

Sesame carrots: drain and rinse the carrots and splash with the remaining soy sauce and the sesame oil. When ready to use, drain and garnish with a pinch of toasted sesame seeds.

Spicy mayo sauce: mix together the sriracha sauce and mayo and set aside.

Pickled egg pearl barley: drain, rinse and dry the pearl barley (I tip it onto a kitchen towel). Mix the mint, coriander/cilantro and grated egg (if using) through the pearl barley and season with olive oil and a pinch of salt and pepper.

Mango: sprinkle the juice and zest of 1 lime over the mango cubes. Season with a pinch of salt and diced red chilli/chile.

Toast the tortillas (if using) in a dry frying pan/skillet for a minute on each side, fold into quarters and set aside. Divide the egg-barley mix between four bowls, then place all other components on top, including the edamame beans. Drizzle over the spicy sauce. Add a lime wedge and fresh herbs, then slot the folded tortilla down the side of each bowl to serve.

MACKEREL & BUTTER BEAN 'ESCABECHE'

Butter beans are a great canned ingredient and ideal used as the backbone for Mediterranean-style recipes like this one that are dressed with tangy vinaigrettes. Here the acidic sherry vinegar and silky olive oil cry out for chunks of good crusty bread to mop them up.

1 large carrot
1 tablespoon coriander seeds, lightly cracked
80 ml/⅓ cup sherry vinegar
80 ml/⅓ cup extra virgin olive oil
2 large garlic cloves, thickly sliced
a sprig of fresh thyme
a pinch of smoked paprika
400-g/14-oz. can butter beans, drained and rinsed
2 x 110-g/4-oz. cans steamed mackerel fillets in olive oil, drained
a few sprigs of fresh flat-leaf parsley
rustic bread, to serve

Serves 2 as a main; 4 as a side

Peel the carrot, then use the potato peeler to shave off a dozen long strips. Place these in a bowl with the coriander seeds and vinegar and leave to steep.

Pour all the olive oil into a small pan, add the garlic, sprig of thyme and pinch of smoked paprika and cook the garlic, over a low heat without burning, for a couple of minutes (just long enough for it to soften).

Drain the vinegar from the carrot strips and pour it into the pan with the garlic, and lightly whisk with a fork.

Gently fold in the butter beans and the mackerel fillets, keeping the mackerel in big chunks.

Transfer to a serving dish or individual bowls and top with the lightly pickled carrot shavings and a scattering of parsley leaves. Serve with rustic bread on the side for mopping up the dressing.

ARBORIO
RISOTTO RICE
biona
IN SALTED WATER
SWEETCORN
IN WATER
NATURALLY SWEET
Harvested at their juiciest
at the peak of the season
446
Del Monte
Quality
SLICES
IN JUICE
BRUNSWICK
Sardines
SARDINES CLUPEA HARENGUS
with hot peppers in soya oil / met hete pepers in sojaolie
mit scharfen Chilischoten in Sojaöl

SKILLETS & STIR-FRIES

EGYPTIAN FAVA BEANS

This delicious brunch dish is packed with protein and full of flavour. I serve mine with hard-boiled/cooked eggs, but if you want to be really indulgent, swap these for a fried egg. You'll need cans of the cooked brown fava beans (sometimes labelled 'ful medames'). If you can't find these, then borlotti/cranberry beans make a good substitute. Serve with toasted pitta breads to mop things up.

2 eggs
2 x 250-g/9-oz. cans broad/fava beans (brown)
1 garlic clove, crushed
a pinch of ground cumin
a pinch of cayenne pepper
½ vegetable stock cube
2 tablespoons extra virgin olive oil
freshly squeezed juice of ½ lemon
a few sprigs of fresh flat-leaf parsley, finely chopped
salt and freshly ground black pepper
toasted pitta breads, to serve (optional)

Serves 2

Place both eggs into a saucepan of water, bring to a simmer and simmer for 5–7 minutes depending on how you like your yolks, then remove and plunge the eggs into cold water so the yolks stay yellow. Leave to cool, before peeling and slicing in half.

While the eggs are cooking, pour the contents of both cans of broad/fava beans into a frying pan/skillet (along with their liquid) and add the garlic, cumin, cayenne pepper, a generous pinch of salt and freshly ground black pepper and then crumble in the stock cube. Add a splash more water if the mixture is dry.

Bring this to a simmer and once it is all piping hot, use a potato masher to break down two-thirds of the beans while they are in the pan – this will make the mixture creamier and thicker. Continue simmering until you have a thick consistency and then remove from the heat.

Place the halved eggs on top of the beans in the pan. Whisk together the olive oil, lemon juice and chopped parsley and drizzle over the contents of the pan before serving.

BLACK BEAN BURGERS

These were a real hit in our household and make for a tasty vegan alternative to traditional burgers. We all like the addition of the corn kernels for texture and a touch of sweetness. They are a bit on the delicate side as I avoided using any egg to bind them (to keep them vegan) so handle them carefully when cooking. Which brings me onto the trimmings – we do cheat a little with the cheese and mayonnaise, but you can of course use plant-based alternatives if preferred.

If you want to serve these with little crispy potato wedges, simply cut up a 570-g/20-oz. can of new potatoes, drizzle with oil, season and roast in the oven at 200°C fan/220°C/425°F/Gas 7 for 40 minutes.

2 onions, diced
a splash of olive oil, for frying
3 garlic cloves, chopped
400-g/14-oz. can black beans, drained and rinsed
200-g/7-oz. can sweetcorn/corn kernels, drained
½ x 400-g/14-oz. can black beluga lentils, drained and rinsed
2 tablespoons smoked paprika
25 g/¼ cup porridge/rolled oats
1 tablespoon plain/all-purpose flour
a few sprigs of fresh coriander/cilantro, chopped
salt and freshly ground black pepper
4 burger-cheese slices (optional)

TO SERVE

4 burger buns, sliced in half (I like the brioche ones)
tomato ketchup
½ iceberg lettuce, shredded
2 vine tomatoes, sliced
mayonnaise

Serves 4

Fry the onions in a splash of olive oil in a frying pan/skillet over a low heat for about 10 minutes, then add the garlic and warm through for another couple of minutes, then remove from the heat.

Tip the beans into a large mixing bowl, mash with the back of a fork until well puréed, or as best as you can do. Tip the sweetcorn/corn kernels onto a chopping board and run a knife over them, just to break them up slightly, then add to the bowl of beans along with the lentils, smoked paprika, oats, flour, coriander/cilantro and cooked onions and garlic. Season very generously with salt and black pepper.

Heat a heavy-based frying pan/skillet and drizzle in a splash of olive oil. Form 4 patties with the burger mixture and place them into the pan – don't move them. Leave them to char on the outside for a few minutes before carefully turning them over. Don't worry if they break up a little. As soon as you've turned them, lay a cheese slice on top (if using) and continue cooking for a few more minutes.

Finally, toast the burger buns on a griddle pan or in a lightly oiled frying pan/skillet, lace with ketchup, place a burger patty on top, followed by a couple of slices of tomato, some lettuce, then mayo and finish with the top of the bun.

FAUX PULLED PORK WITH BLACKENED CORN

My vegan faux 'pulled pork' uses jackfruit and is deliciously smoky and barbecue-y. It's accompanied by blackened corn which is good enough to eat on its own. Serve nacho-style spooned over tortilla chips, with rice, or in a soft bun (if you are not afraid to get dirty!).

2 x 400-g/14-oz. cans jackfruit
a splash of olive oil
1 large onion, thickly sliced
1 tablespoon smoked paprika
1 tablespoon ground cumin
1 teaspoon plain/all-purpose flour
80 ml/5½ tablespoons tomato ketchup
1 teaspoon dark soy sauce
1 tablespoon maple syrup
1 teaspoon cider vinegar
a generous pinch of dried oregano
200-g/7-oz. can sweetcorn/corn kernels, drained
a small pinch of cayenne pepper
sea salt flakes and freshly ground black pepper

TO SERVE
tortilla chips, rice or a burger bun
sliced fresh or pickled chillies/chiles
lime wedges, for squeezing

Serves 4

Drain the jackfruit through a sieve/strainer, pushing it down to release the excess water. Just before you are ready to use it, pat it dry with paper towels.

Heat a frying pan/skillet to smoking hot, add a splash of olive oil and stir-fry the onion for a minute to char, then immediately turn off the heat and remove the onion from the pan (you want the onion to remain slightly firm).

Mix the paprika, cumin and flour together in a bowl and toss the jackfruit in to coat. Reheat the skillet, add another splash of oil if needed and fry the jackfruit for a few minutes to get some colour. Using the back of a fork or a potato masher, gently push down to break up the jackfruit slightly and then add 100 ml/scant ½ cup hot water. Gently shake the pan to mix in the water, then add the ketchup, soy sauce, maple syrup, vinegar and oregano and season with salt flakes and freshly ground black pepper. Simmer over a low heat for a few minutes, breaking up the jackfruit more if needed, until the sauce thickens and becomes glossy. Remove from the heat, scatter the onion over the jackfruit and keep warm.

Heat a clean, dry frying pan/skillet to almost smoking hot. Tip in the sweetcorn/corn kernels, shaking the pan to level them and leave to char for a couple of minutes. Any water will quickly evaporate. As the kernels start to blacken, shake the pan to get an even charring. Remove from the heat, season well with salt flakes and a pinch of cayenne pepper. Serve with the faux pulled pork and trimmings.

SARDINE HOAGIES WITH PICKLED RED ONION

These little pocket rockets are sardine, Parmesan and potato croquettes in a mini sub roll, topped with quick-pickled red onion and peppery rocket/arugula. You can serve the patties on their own, but I like to serve mine this way, with a spicy mayo on the side.

90-g/3-oz. can new potatoes, drained
2 x 90-g/3-oz. cans sardines in oil (you need boneless ones here)
12 g/½ oz. fresh flat-leaf parsley, chopped
30 g/⅓ cup grated Parmesan cheese
½ teaspoon cayenne pepper
2 tablespoons plain/all-purpose flour
a splash of olive oil, for frying
100 g/2 cups fresh breadcrumbs
salt and freshly ground black pepper

SPICY MAYO
100 g/½ cup mayonnaise
2 tablespoons any hot sauce, such as Tabasco
1 teaspoon Worcestershire sauce
a few sprigs of fresh coriander/cilantro, finely chopped

QUICK-PICKLED ONION
½ red onion, very thinly sliced
4 tablespoons cider vinegar
½ teaspoon sugar

TO SERVE
4 mini sub rolls
a handful of rocket/arugula

Serves 4

Mix together all the spicy mayo ingredients and set aside.

For the quick-pickled onion, place the sliced red onion in a small bowl, pour the vinegar and sugar over and leave to steep while you make the patties.

Place the potatoes in a bowl and mash with the back of a fork. Drain and discard some of the excess oil from the sardines, then crumble the sardines into the potatoes (a little bit of oil going into the bowl is okay). Add the parsley, Parmesan and cayenne pepper and season generously with salt and ground black pepper, then mix everything together. Finally, sprinkle over the flour to help bind the mixture.

Tip the breadcrumbs onto a plate. Take golf ball-sized portions of the mixture and form into croquettes, then press into the breadcrumbs to coat on all sides. The croquettes will have quite a soft texture. Heat a splash of oil in a frying pan/skillet and fry the croquettes on both sides for a few minutes until crisp (you may need to do this in batches).

Split the sub rolls lengthways and lightly toast the cut sides. Spread some spicy mayo over each one, add a little rocket/arugula and drop in a couple of croquettes. Finish with the quick-pickled onion. Serve the remaining spicy mayo on the side for dipping.

PAPS' SPEEDY 'N' SPICY CURRY SKILLET

'So, Paps, I'm writing a book on canned food,' I said. 'That's funny, I've just cooked lunch using canned sardines and potatoes,' came his response. 'Perfect!' I said, 'Give me the recipe!'. Well, my dad's quick lunchtime rustle-up turned out to be just great, so here it is...

Also, one thing I've learnt is that canned potatoes won't crisp up unless you dust them in a little flour and fry them, so I've done that here just to give them a little pleasing crunch.

570-g/20-oz. can new potatoes, drained and cut into 2.5-cm/1-inch cubes
plain/all-purpose flour, for dusting
60 ml/4 tablespoons olive oil
1 onion, sliced
12 curry leaves
1 tablespoon coriander seeds
1 dried whole red chilli/chile
1 teaspoon mustard seeds
290-g/10-oz. can garden peas, drained
1 heaped tablespoon any curry powder
2 x 168-g/6-oz. cans sardines, drained
fresh coriander/cilantro, to garnish
1 fresh red chilli/chile, sliced, to garnish
salt and freshly ground black pepper

Serves 4

Dust the diced potatoes in some flour and set aside.

Heat the olive oil in a frying pan/skillet, add the onion, curry leaves, coriander seeds and the whole dried chilli/chile and fry over a medium heat for a couple of minutes until aromatic. Shake off the excess flour from the potatoes (I put them in a sieve/strainer and give it a shake) and add the potatoes and mustard seeds to the pan at the same time.

Gently shake the pan to even out the potatoes, then leave to cook for a minute before moving them around and stir-frying the potatoes until they have gone slightly crispy. You may need to add a splash more oil to the pan.

Add the drained peas to the pan along with the curry powder, salt and black pepper and stir-fry for a minute. Finally, drop the drained sardines into the pan whole and fold them through (they will break up a little which is fine). Once warmed through, remove from the heat and garnish with fresh coriander/cilantro and sliced red chilli/chile.

CORNED BEEF SHAKSHUKA

I remember having corned beef hash as a kid, and this recipe is really a fusion of that throw-back brunch with the more recent darling of brunch menus, the 'shakshuka' (with good reason, it's delicious). A little crumbled feta over the top just as it comes out of the oven is nice if you fancy it.

360-g/13-oz. can new potatoes, cut into 2.5-cm/1-inch cubes
1 red onion, diced
½ small fresh red chilli/chile, chopped
a splash of olive oil, plus extra for drizzling
1 tablespoon Worcestershire sauce
a pinch of ground cumin
200-g/7-oz. can corned beef, roughly chopped
½ x 400-g/14-oz. can cherry tomatoes (about 12 tomatoes plus some juice)
4 eggs
a handful of chopped flat-leaf parsley, to garnish
100 g/¾ cup crumbled feta cheese, to serve (optional)
salt and freshly ground black pepper

Serves 4

Preheat the oven to 200°C fan/220°C/425°F/Gas 7.

Fry the potatoes, onion and chopped chilli/chile in a splash of olive oil in a large ovenproof frying pan/skillet for a couple minutes over a high heat (the potatoes won't take on any colour, but that's okay). Once the onion has softened, sprinkle in the Worcestershire sauce and ground cumin and season generously with freshly ground black pepper and a small pinch of salt.

Fold in the corned beef, breaking it up a little in the pan and incorporating it into the other ingredients. Dot the cherry tomatoes around the pan and drizzle over a couple of tablespoons of the juice.

Make four small 'pockets' in the mixture and crack an egg into each one, leave on the heat for a minute to help cook the undersides of the eggs, drizzle over some olive oil, then place the whole pan in the preheated oven for 6 minutes or until the tops of the eggs have just solidified.

Remove the pan from the oven (remember the handle will be hot!), garnish with chopped parsley and serve straight away at the table. If you wish, crumble the feta over the top just before serving to give a nice contrast to the dish.

ACKEE & ALBACORE TUNA SKILLET
WITH GRIDDLED PINEAPPLE

This is my canned homage to Jamaica's national dish of ackee and saltfish. Canned ackee is a bit delicate so goes into the pan at the very end of cooking to avoid any damage. I've used Scotch bonnet chilli/chile in keeping with the Jamaican theme, but feel free to use a milder variety if you like.

½ x 200-g/7-oz. can pork luncheon meat, such as Spam
a splash of olive oil
1 red onion, diced
2 garlic cloves, sliced
a generous pinch of dried thyme
1 Scotch bonnet chilli/chile, seeds removed, finely chopped
½ x 400-g/14-oz. can cherry tomatoes, drained
½ teaspoon ground allspice
½ x 400-g/14-oz. jar roasted red (bell) peppers, drained and sliced
2 spring onions/scallions, sliced
2 x 160-g/5¾-oz. cans albacore tuna fillets in oil, drained
280-g/10-oz. can ackee, drained
220-g/8-oz. can pineapple rings in natural juice
a few sprigs of fresh coriander/cilantro, finely chopped
1 lime, cut into 6 wedges
salt and freshly ground black pepper
a few slices of toasted rustic bread, cut into large fingers, to serve

Serves 4

Finely dice the luncheon meat and fry in a heavy-based saucepan with a splash of oil over a high heat for a few minutes until it browns and starts to crisp; if there is a lot of oil in the pan, discard some, but ensure a tablespoon remains.

Add the diced onion and sweat for a couple of minutes until softened, then add the garlic, thyme and half the chopped chilli/chile. After a minute add the tomatoes, allspice, jarred peppers and spring onions/scallions (saving a pinch for the pineapple). Season with ½ teaspoon salt and bring to a simmer. After a minute gently flake in the tuna, keeping it quite chunky, and then carefully fold in the ackee and leave to get hot. Once hot, remove from the heat and keep warm.

Drain the pineapple slices, pat dry with paper towels and season with salt and black pepper. Bring a dry griddle pan to almost smoking hot and then place the pineapple rings onto the griddle; leave for a couple of minutes, then once charred, turn over and cook for another minute or two. Lay the pineapple slices on a plate, sprinkle over some chopped coriander/cilantro, a pinch of Scotch bonnet, the leftover spring onions/scallions and a squeeze of lime juice.

Scatter the remaining chopped coriander/cilantro over the warm tuna and ackee mixture and add a squeeze of lime juice. Serve with the griddled pineapple, lime wedges and toasted rustic bread to mop up the juices.

SUCCOTASH

There's something very pleasing about saying the word 'succotash' and it is equally satisfying to eat. My take on this noble dish of corn and beans with a long history is one of those 'if you've got it, add it' recipes, which makes it great for sneaking in any leftovers you want to use up. Start by frying the diced luncheon meat so it resembles crispy bacon – seriously, it's a great canned alternative!

400-g/14-oz. can cherry tomatoes
2 x 300-g/10½-oz. cans broad/fava beans
400-g/14-oz can butter beans
325-g/11½-oz. can sweetcorn/corn kernels
200-g/7-oz. can pork luncheon meat, such as Spam
1 tablespoon olive oil
1 onion, diced
2 garlic cloves, sliced
1 teaspoon maple syrup
2 tablespoons cider vinegar
a knob/pat of butter
a few sprigs of fresh flat-leaf parsley, chopped
a few sprigs of fresh basil, torn
1 fresh or pickled green chilli/chile, sliced
salt and freshly ground black pepper

Serves 4

Prepare all the canned vegetables by draining them and leaving to one side ready to use, including the whole cherry tomatoes (you can save the tomato juice to use in another recipe).

Slice the pork luncheon meat into thin 3-mm/⅛-inch strips, then dice and fry in a large hot frying pan/skillet with the oil until dark and crisp – this will take about 8 minutes (don't take it out earlier – it must be crispy). Remove the luncheon meat and place on paper towels, leaving a couple of tablespoons of the rendered fat behind.

Fry the diced onion in the frying pan/skillet for about 5 minutes until softened, then add the garlic and stir through for a minute. Add the tomatoes, beans, sweetcorn/corn kernels, maple syrup and vinegar. Season with freshly ground black pepper and a pinch of salt and cook for a few minutes until the ingredients are hot and most of the liquid has evaporated.

Finish with a knob/pat of butter, the fresh herbs and a few slices of chilli/chile, and finally, sprinkle the crispy pork luncheon meat pieces over the top.

SPAM & CHEESE FRITTERS IN COLA TEMPURA

This retro dish of luncheon meat fritters has had an upgrade. I sandwich slices of it around a melting cheese middle and cook it in a cola tempura batter which gives it a subtle sweetness and plenty of crunch. All this and then the hot fritters are dipped into a fiery red pepper sauce!

200-g/7-oz. can pork luncheon meat, such as Spam
100 g/3½ oz. Cheddar cheese
130 g/1 cup self-raising/rising flour
50 g/½ cup cornflour/cornstarch
about 150 ml/⅔ cup cola
vegetable oil, for frying

RED PEPPER SAUCE
1 tablespoon tomato purée/paste
a pinch of sugar
½ fresh red or pickled chilli/chile
½ garlic clove
100 g/3½ oz. roasted red peppers from a jar or can, drained and chopped
2 tablespoons olive oil
1 teaspoon cider vinegar
salt

Serves 4 to share

Make the sauce by adding all the ingredients except the olive oil and vinegar to a food processor (or finely chop and mix using a pestle and mortar), pulse together, add a pinch of salt and whisk in the olive oil and vinegar (omit the vinegar if the roasted peppers are already in an acidic brine). Set aside.

Cut the pork luncheon meat and the cheese into slices about 3 mm/⅛ inch thick (the cheese needs to be the same size as the slices of meat, and you need twice the number of meat slices as cheese), then sandwich each slice of cheese between two slices of meat.

Pour the vegetable oil into a large saucepan or deep frying pan/skillet to a depth of least 2.5 cm/1 inch and heat.

Place half the self-raising/rising flour on a plate and put to one side. In a mixing bowl, combine the remaining flour with the cornflour/cornstarch and whisk in just under 150 ml/⅔ cup cola to form a lumpy batter; add more cola if it's too thick (you want the consistency of double/heavy cream), but don't over whisk.

When the oil is hot enough (test by dropping a dot of batter into the oil – it should sizzle immediately but take 30 seconds to colour), take one 'sandwich', dust in flour, then coat in the batter. Scoop out of the batter with a fork and place into the hot oil. Cook for a couple of minutes on each side or until crisp and golden, then remove and drain on paper towels. Continue until all the fritters are cooked, then serve with the red pepper sauce on the side.

HAM & CHEESE TORTILLA WITH PIQUANTÉ SALSA

I love the convenience of using canned potatoes and ham to whip up this tasty Spanish-style tortilla in half the time it would usually take, and the best bit is no one even knows I've taken a few shortcuts!

a splash of olive oil
1 large red onion, sliced
4 eggs
60 g/⅔ cup grated/shredded Cheddar cheese
a sprig of fresh flat-leaf parsley, chopped
200-g/7-oz. can Danish ham, cut into 1-cm/½-inch cubes
360-g/13-oz. can new potatoes, drained and cut into 5-mm/¼-inch thick slices
15 g/1 tablespoon butter
salt and freshly ground black pepper
rustic bread, to serve

PIQUANTÉ PEPPER SALSA
100-g/3½-oz. jar piquanté peppers, drained (reserve the juice)
a few slices of red onion (reserved from making the tortilla)
a sprig of fresh flat-leaf parsley, chopped
1 tablespoon tomato purée/paste
sugar or honey, to taste
2 tablespoons olive oil

20-cm/8-inch ovenproof frying pan/skillet

Serves 4

Preheat the oven to 200°C fan/220°C/425°F/Gas 7.

Heat a splash of olive oil in the frying pan/skillet. Set aside a few onion slices for the salsa; add the rest to the pan and fry over a low heat for about 8 minutes until soft and golden.

Whisk the eggs in a bowl and fold through the grated cheese and chopped parsley. Once the onion is ready, fold it into the bowl of whisked eggs. Using the same pan, fry the ham for a few minutes to give it a little colour, then add the potatoes to warm them through. Season generously, then fold them into the eggs as well.

Wipe the pan if it is sticky. Add the butter, return the pan to the heat and, once foaming, pour in the egg mixture. Leave to cook for a few minutes until you can pull the edges of the tortilla away from the edge of the pan a little (it will still be raw on top), then pop into the preheated oven for 5 minutes.

Remove the pan from the oven, place a plate on top and holding the plate in place, flip the pan over so the tortilla rests upside down on the plate. Now slide it back into the pan (you've flipped the tortilla to cook the top of it in the pan). Cook for a few more minutes in the oven, then leave to rest while you make the salsa.

To make the salsa, dice the piquanté peppers, reserved onion and parsley and mix together in a bowl. Stir in the tomato purée/paste, olive oil, plus a tablespoon of juice from the jar of peppers. Sweeten to taste with sugar or honey. Serve the tortilla in slices with a little of the salsa spooned over the top and with rustic bread on the side.

MR WEI'S SWEET & SOUR CHICKEN

Travelling through China, my girlfriend (it's okay, she's my wife now) and I stayed at a hostel in the Guilin Province owned by Mr Wei. He showed us how to cook an authentic sweet and sour chicken dish. This recipe is inspired by that dish, but about as inauthentic as could be! Top tip: chop, dice and prepare everything before you start cooking.

425-g/15-oz. can mango pieces in syrup
1 tablespoon cornflour/cornstarch
2 tablespoons rice vinegar (or any other vinegar except balsamic)
1 large egg
200-g/7-oz. can chicken breast, drained, rinsed and cut into 1-cm/½-inch cubes
200 g/1½ cups plain/all-purpose flour
350 ml/1½ cups vegetable oil
a splash of olive oil
1 large onion, thickly sliced
1 fresh red (bell) pepper, deseeded and cut into bite-sized pieces
2 garlic cloves, chopped
5-cm/2-inch piece of fresh ginger, peeled and diced
1 fresh red chilli/chile, sliced
225-g/8-oz. can sliced water chestnuts, drained
2 tablespoons soy sauce, plus extra for drizzling
a few sprigs of fresh coriander/cilantro, chopped, to garnish
salt
boiled rice, to serve

Serves 4

Drain the mango, reserving the syrup – you should have about 250 ml/1 cup plus 1 tablespoon; if not, top up with a splash of water. Whisk the cornflour/cornstarch and vinegar into the syrup. Slice the mango into 5-cm/2-inch pieces.

Whisk the egg in a bowl and set aside. Dust the diced canned chicken breast in flour, then dip into the egg wash, then back into the flour until fully coated and all pieces are separated.

Heat the vegetable oil in a large saucepan; it's hot enough when a cube of chicken sizzles immediately when you drop it in and turns golden in about 30 seconds. Deep fry the chicken pieces in batches until they are lightly golden, then drain on paper towels; season with salt and set aside.

In a separate, very hot pan, add a splash of olive oil and stir-fry the onion and (bell) pepper for a couple of minutes until you see some brown tinges. Add the garlic, ginger and chilli/chile, stirring frequently for another minute, then add the drained water chestnuts and soy sauce and season with salt.

Reduce the heat to medium and pour in the mango syrup, shaking the pan as you do. It will start to thicken immediately. As it thickens, fold in the chicken and then the mango. Once the mango is in, try not to stir too much as the mango will break up; just leave to warm through for a minute. Garnish with chopped coriander/cilantro and an extra drizzle of soy sauce over the top, and serve with rice.

Organico

PASTA, NOODLES & RICE

TRAY-BAKED SPAGHETTI PUTTANESCA

The concept behind this tray-bake recipe was born out of the live kids-cookalongs for families I started online in 2020 and it proved to be one of our most popular dishes with viewers – and with good reason! It's the ultimate in convenience cooking as everything just goes into the sheet pan (yes, even the dried spaghetti!) and 30 minutes later dinner is served!

320 g/11½ oz. dried spaghetti
1 onion, diced
3 garlic cloves, sliced
90-g/3¼-oz. can pitted/stoned black olives, drained and halved
2 tablespoons capers, coarsely chopped
15 g/2 tablespoons raisins
a pinch of chilli/hot red pepper flakes (optional)
60 ml/4 tablespoons olive oil
400-g/14-oz. can cherry tomatoes
1 tablespoon tomato purée/paste
650 ml/2¾ cups warm chicken stock (made with 1 stock cube)
155-g/5½-oz. can pilchards in tomato sauce
a few sprigs of fresh flat-leaf parsley, chopped
salt and freshly ground black pepper

High-sided sheet/roasting pan

Serves 4

Preheat the oven to 200°C fan/220°C/425°F/Gas 7.

Lay the spaghetti in the high-sided sheet/roasting pan with all the dry ingredients – onion, garlic, olives, capers, raisins, chilli/hot red pepper flakes – then pour in the olive oil, massaging it over the spaghetti to ensure it is coated. Then add all the wet ingredients – the cherry tomatoes in their sauce, tomato purée/paste, warm chicken stock, pilchards in their sauce – and season with salt and black pepper. Use a fork to mix all the ingredients together, breaking the pilchards up a little as you do (but keep them fairly chunky). The spaghetti should be submerged below the liquid by about 1 cm/½ inch.

Place the pan in the preheated oven and bake for 30 minutes, then remove and leave to rest for 5 minutes – this stage is important as it allows the bake to finish cooking and absorb the last of the liquid. Once done, use a fork to loosen the spaghetti and garnish with freshly chopped parsley. If it's too thick, feel free to add a splash of hot water, or if too loose, leave it in the oven for another 5 minutes.

SIMPLE SPAGHETTI WITH ANCHOVY & LEMON

This is one of those recipes that is so much more than the sum of its parts, and once tried you'll keep coming back to it. In Italy a simple pasta dish like this would be served with a sprinkling of seasoned fried breadcrumbs, but some bread on the side works just as well.

320 g/11½ oz. dried spaghetti
50-g/1¾-oz. can anchovies in olive oil
2 tablespoons extra virgin olive oil
3 garlic cloves, thinly sliced
finely grated zest and freshly squeezed juice of 1 lemon
a few sprigs of fresh flat-leaf parsley, chopped
a pinch of chilli/hot red pepper flakes
salt and freshly ground black pepper
rustic bread, to serve

Serves 4

Start by cooking the spaghetti in a pan of lightly salted boiling water following the package instructions; for al dente it's usually about 8 minutes.

Meanwhile, open the can of anchovies and tip the whole can (including the olive oil) into a medium-hot pan along with the extra virgin olive oil and the garlic. Cook gently, prodding occasionally, until the anchovies have dissolved and the garlic is aromatic (but not burnt). Squeeze in the lemon juice and add the chopped parsley and stir to incorporate. Remove from the heat until the pasta is cooked.

Once the pasta is done, use a pair of tongs to pull the pasta from the saucepan into the anchovy pan, allowing some of the salted cooking water to go in with it. Turn the heat on and pull the spaghetti up and down in the pan to absorb all those lovely flavours and to help emulsify the oils with the starch of the cooking liquid. Season with freshly ground black pepper and a pinch of chilli/hot red pepper flakes and finish with a few grates of lemon zest. Serve with rustic bread on the side.

EVA'S SMOKED SEAFOOD TAGLIATELLE

My daughter Eva loves a seafood pasta and this recipe is dedicated to her. She is a gorgeous little force of nature who generally acts more like an adult than I do! This simple dish is really a vehicle for the mussels which give an instant depth of flavour, along with the oil from the can which they have infused with their smokiness. I always add canned squid too, as it works well alongside the mussels.

85-g/3-oz. can smoked mussels in oil
2 garlic cloves, sliced
400-g/14-oz can cherry tomatoes
a pinch of sugar
a very small pinch of chilli/hot red pepper flakes
½ teaspoon ground cinnamon
250 g/9 oz. dried tagliatelle or spaghetti
2 x 110-g/4-oz. cans squid in oil, drained
a few sprigs of fresh flat-leaf parsley or coriander/cilantro, chopped
sea salt flakes and freshly ground black pepper

Serves 4

Pour the oil from the can of mussels into a pan and gently warm the sliced garlic for a couple of minutes. Partly open the can of cherry tomatoes, drain off about half the juice (save the drained juice for another recipe) and tip the remaining tomatoes and juice into the pan. Add the sugar, chilli/hot red pepper flakes and cinnamon. Leave the pan on a low simmer with the lid off to reduce and cook out the acidity of the tomatoes.

While the sauce is simmering, cook the tagliatelle in a pan of salted boiling water following the packet instructions for al dente – about 8 minutes.

Just before the pasta is cooked, add the smoked mussels and the squid to the pan of sauce (no need to add the oil from the squid) and fold it all together, seasoning with freshly ground black pepper and a pinch of sea salt flakes.

Finally, using a pair of tongs, pull the pasta from the pot and place into the pan with the sauce, lift it a couple of times to incorporate, then leave on the heat for another minute to help the pasta absorb all those delicious flavours. Serve with a scattering of parsley or coriander/ cilantro over the top; sometimes I give it a drizzle of olive oil too.

CREAMY TOMATO & TUNA PASTA BAKE

What self-respecting canned cookbook wouldn't include a proper store-cupboard tuna pasta bake/casserole? Not this one, that's for sure! I love how the cream of tomato soup softens the sauce, making it a little creamier than using regular canned tomatoes; plus it's really quick – you just need to put it together and whack it in the oven! And to ring the changes, this recipe works equally well using cream of mushroom or asparagus soup (just leave out the tomato purée/paste).

360 g/12½ oz. dried fusilli or penne pasta
a splash of olive oil
1 onion, diced
2 garlic cloves, chopped
2 tablespoons tomato purée/paste
2 teaspoons dried mixed herbs or dried oregano
½ x 150-g/5½-oz. can pitted/stoned black olives, drained
400-g/14-oz. can cream of tomato soup
110-g/4-oz. can tuna, drained
100 g/1 cup grated/shredded Cheddar cheese
150-g/5½-oz. mozzarella ball
salt and freshly ground black pepper

Serves 4

Preheat the oven to 200°C fan/220°C/425°F/Gas 7.

Cook the pasta in a pan of salted boiling water for about 8 minutes (under-cook it by a minute or two). Drain, reserving 125 ml/½ cup of the cooking water.

Meanwhile, heat a splash of olive oil in a large ovenproof pan and fry the onion for a few minutes until softened, then stir in the garlic for a moment. Follow this with the tomato purée/paste, dried herbs, olives and a generous seasoning of salt and freshly ground black pepper.

Pour in the can of soup, stir and let it simmer gently for a few minutes. Tip the drained pasta into the sauce and stir to incorporate fully, then add the reserved pasta cooking water. Crumble in the tuna, folding it in just enough to be fully coated – you don't want it obliterated in the sauce.

Scatter the grated Cheddar all over the top, then cut the mozzarella into five or six slices and lay them over the top. Finish with a little drizzle of olive oil.

Pop into the preheated oven for 10 minutes or until the cheese has fully melted, then serve.

UPSIDE-DOWN CHICKEN & PRUNE TAGINE

This is a recipe that always makes me smile – all the deliciously rich flavours you'd expect from a tagine (one-pot Moroccan stew), but here the traditional accompaniment of couscous is cooked in the pot at the same time. How neat is that? If you're feeling brave, place a large plate on top of the pan and try flipping the whole thing over so the couscous is underneath the stew when you serve it. That said, I don't bother unless I'm cooking for friends and want to show off!

400-g/14-oz. can prunes in natural juice
30 ml/2 tablespoons olive oil
1 red onion, sliced
2 x 200-g/7-oz. cans chicken breast, drained, rinsed and cut into wedges
3 garlic cloves, sliced
285-g/10-oz. jar roasted red (bell) peppers, drained, rinsed and sliced
½ x 400-g/14-oz. can chopped tomatoes
1 tablespoon smoked paprika
1 teaspoon ground cumin
1 teaspoon ground cinnamon
1 tablespoon dried oregano
a pinch of chilli/hot red pepper flakes
1 teaspoon runny honey
1 chicken stock cube
180 g/1 cup couscous
2 tablespoons toasted flaked/slivered almonds
3 tablespoons freshly chopped flat-leaf parsley
salt and freshly ground black pepper

Serves 4

Drain the prunes, reserving 60 ml/4 tablespoons of the juice. Discard the pits/stones.

Heat the oil in a large frying pan/skillet, add the onion and fry for a few minutes until softened. Then add the chicken chunks and fry for another minute before adding the garlic and roasted peppers. Continue frying for a couple of minutes, then add the tomatoes, all the spices, oregano, chilli/red hot pepper flakes, honey and salt and pepper and simmer for 5 minutes. Add the prunes and reserved juice and crumble in the stock cube – the mixture should be quite thick at this stage.

Turn the heat down to low and shake the pan to level the top (or use the back of a spoon), then scatter the couscous straight over the top as evenly as you can, covering the entire pan. Carefully pour about 500 ml/ 2 cups hot water over the couscous and place a tight-fitting lid on top of the pan (use foil if you don't have a lid or if it's an ill-fitting one). Leave to cook over a very low heat for about 10 minutes, then turn off the heat, leave the lid on and rest for a further 5 minutes. (If you are going to flip it over, now is the time.) Remove the lid, garnish with the flaked/slivered almonds, chopped parsley and a pinch of salt, and serve.

CHICKEN RAMEN

A good ramen soup is quite a production to put together, requiring a rich stock made over several hours. However, this quick version is ideal when you want a fast noodle fix and is made with ingredients that can be found in your kitchen. The soup cools quickly so it's a good idea to warm your bowls before serving (I just pour a little hot water from the kettle into them). If you want to make this a little more substantial, you can add a can of drained whole button mushrooms.

4 eggs
250 g/9 oz. dried egg noodles
1 tablespoon olive oil
1 tablespoon sesame oil
1 garlic clove, very finely sliced
5-cm/2-inch piece of fresh ginger, peeled and finely diced
750 ml/3¼ cups chicken stock (made with 2 stock cubes)
2 tablespoons dark soy sauce
1 tablespoon light soy sauce
a pinch of sugar
2 x 200-g/7-oz. cans chicken breast, drained and rinsed
325-g/11½-oz. can sweetcorn/corn kernels, drained
a few sprigs of fresh coriander/cilantro, roughly chopped
1 fresh red chilli/chile, sliced
1 lime, cut into wedges
toasted sesame seeds, to garnish
salt

Serves 4

Place the eggs in a saucepan of salted boiling water; after 2 minutes add the noodles and cook according to the packet instructions (about 5 minutes). Once cooked, remove the eggs, plunge them into a bowl of cold water (this will keep the yolks bright yellow) and set aside. Drain the noodles and mix them with half the olive oil to stop them sticking. Peel the eggs and cut in half.

Pour the sesame oil and remaining olive oil into a large saucepan and warm the garlic and ginger for a minute, then pour in the chicken stock, soy sauces, sugar and a pinch of salt. Bring to a simmer.

Cut the chicken breast into neat slices and drop into the saucepan to warm through for a couple of minutes. Divide the noodles amongst the serving bowls, then using a slotted spoon remove the chicken breast slices and place on top of the noodles in the bowls. Tip the sweetcorn/corn kernels into the saucepan to warm for a few seconds, then remove with a slotted spoon and divide amongst the bowls.

Finally, pour the bubbling soup over the noodles in each bowl, top with chopped coriander/cilantro and the eggs, and garnish with sliced chilli/chile, a wedge of lime and a sprinkling of toasted sesame seeds. Serve immediately.

SINGAPORE NOODLES

Vermicelli rice noodles stir-fried with mixed Chinese vegetables and seasoned with that trademark hint of Indian curry spice makes Singapore-style noodles a sure-fire winner every time. I find a little sweet chilli sauce drizzled over the top to serve works really well.

2 x 400-g/14-oz. cans Chinese mixed vegetables
OR
120-g/4¼-oz. can bamboo shoots, 140-g/5-oz. can sliced water chestnuts and 160-g/5¾-oz. can baby sweetcorn/corn or bean shoots
250 g/9 oz. vermicelli rice noodles
2 tablespoons medium curry powder
½ teaspoon ground turmeric
about 2 tablespoons vegetable oil
3 eggs, lightly beaten
1 onion, cut into 1-cm/½-inch thick slices
4 garlic cloves, sliced
1 tablespoon sesame oil
2 tablespoons dark soy sauce
a pinch of sugar
a few sprigs of fresh coriander/cilantro, chopped
sweet chilli/chili sauce, to serve (optional)

Serves 4

Drain and rinse the canned vegetables, then leave in a sieve/strainer above a bowl while you prepare the rest of the dish.

Submerge the noodles in a bowl of just-boiled water, leave for about 6–8 minutes or until hydrated but still a little al dente. Drain, rinse under cold water and leave to drip-dry in a separate sieve/strainer. Run a knife once through the noodles to break them down a little, then dust with the curry powder and turmeric.

Add a splash of vegetable oil to a frying pan/skillet. When hot, add the beaten eggs and quickly fry, then transfer to a bowl and set aside.

Reheat the frying pan/skillet until almost smoking, add the remaining vegetable oil and the onion and stir-fry for a few minutes, then add the garlic, stir-fry for another 30 seconds, then add the canned vegetables and continue to stir-fry over a high heat for a minute. Pour in the sesame oil, then add the noodles, eggs, soy sauce and a pinch of sugar. Keep lifting the noodles to incorporate all the ingredients and once piping hot, remove from the heat. Serve with a few fresh coriander/cilantro leaves scattered over the top.

KOWLOON RICE POT

This recipe is inspired by the claypot rice dishes of Kowloon's Temple Street night market in Hong Kong, where you find rice cooked in little clay pots over charcoal with dozens of toppings to choose from. The beauty is that everything is cooked in the one pot, so when you dig into it you find pockets of plain rice and others where the toppings and dressing have soaked through to give it a delicious smoky flavour.

1 tablespoon olive oil
1 tablespoon sesame oil
1 onion, diced
2 garlic cloves, chopped
250 g/1½ cups basmati rice
290-g/10-oz. can petit pois, drained
1 teaspoon smoked paprika
600 ml/2½ cups chicken stock (made with 1 stock cube)
2 x 200-g/7-oz. cans chicken breast, drained and rinsed
400-g/14-oz. can beansprouts, drained
1 spring onion/scallion, thinly sliced
salt

DRESSING

4 tablespoons dark soy sauce
2 tablespoons runny honey
1 teaspoon cider vinegar
1 tablespoon tomato purée/paste
5-cm/2-inch piece of fresh ginger, peeled and grated
½ teaspoon Chinese five spice
a pinch of chilli/hot red pepper flakes

Serves 4

Mix all the dressing ingredients together and set aside.

Add the oils to a saucepan and fry the onion for a few minutes to soften, then add the garlic and cook for 30 seconds. Stir in the rice, petit pois, smoked paprika and a pinch of salt and top with the chicken stock. Bring to the boil, then reduce the heat to low, cover with a lid and cook for 10 minutes.

While the rice is cooking, cut the chicken breast into 1-cm/½-inch thick slices. Drain the beansprouts in a sieve/strainer, shaking off as much excess liquid as possible.

After 10 minutes of cooking, quickly remove the lid from the pan and spread the beansprouts in a layer on top of the rice and sprinkle a third of the dressing over the beansprouts, then fan out the chicken slices over the top of the beansprouts and replace the lid. Continue cooking for another 3 minutes, then remove from the heat and rest for 5 minutes with the lid on before serving.

Just before serving, drizzle over all the remaining dressing and garnish with the sliced spring onion/scallion.

LUCA'S CREAMY MUSHROOM RISOTTO

This is Luca's mushroom risotto – he's the youngest in our family and the only four-year-old I know who loves mushrooms! My easy recipe uses mushroom soup as a stock, and I found roasting the canned mushrooms changed their texture and intensified the flavour. A few grates of Parmesan cheese folded in just before serving and some extra over the top to garnish is a really nice touch. You can use a vegetarian alternative to the cheese, if you prefer.

2 x 285-g/10-oz. cans whole button mushrooms, drained
2 tablespoons olive oil, plus extra for drizzling
1 onion, diced
2 garlic cloves, chopped
200 g/1 heaped cup arborio rice
400-g/14-oz. can cream of mushroom soup
1 vegetable or chicken stock cube
a sprig of fresh thyme (or 1 teaspoon dried thyme)
30 g/2 tablespoons butter
1 teaspoon freshly squeezed lemon juice
salt and freshly ground black pepper
freshly grated Parmesan cheese, to serve (optional)

Serves 4

Preheat the oven to 200°C fan/220°C/425°F/Gas 7.

Drain the mushrooms, gently squeezing them to release some of their liquid. Cut any large ones in half. Line a baking sheet with parchment paper, scatter the mushrooms over the paper, season and then bake in the preheated oven for about 25 minutes, then remove and set aside. They'll dry out, shrink and have a much more intense mushroom flavour.

Meanwhile, heat the oil in a saucepan, add the onion and fry for a few minutes to soften. Add the garlic and cook for 30 seconds. Add the rice, fry for another minute, then pour in 250 ml/1 cup of the mushroom soup and 500 ml/2 cups hot water. Crumble in the stock cube and add the thyme.

Simmer over a low heat, stirring frequently, for about 20 minutes (give or take 5 minutes). Top up with more hot water if needed, tasting towards the end to test if the rice is cooked – it should be soft but still with a little chew.

Season very generously with salt and pepper and remove from the heat to rest for a minute (remove the sprig of thyme if used). While resting, fold in half the roasted mushrooms, the butter, lemon juice and the remaining mushroom soup (add another splash of hot water if it's too thick).

Serve in bowls, topped with the remaining roasted mushrooms, a drizzle of olive oil and Parmesan, if using.

EASY SEAFOOD & CHICKEN RICE

This dish is inspired by a classic Spanish paella, but I've used basmati rice to reduce the cooking time. The communal aspect of eating a paella is something I love – a big pan placed in the middle of the table and everyone helping themselves. I use a mix of seafood and chicken and like to serve it with a crisp green salad on the side.

1 onion, diced
60 ml/4 tablespoons olive oil
2 garlic cloves, sliced
285-g/10-oz. jar roasted red peppers, drained and half roughly chopped, half cut into strips
2 tablespoons smoked paprika
a pinch of ground turmeric
3 tablespoons tomato purée/paste
250 g/1½ cups basmati rice
400-g/14-oz. can green beans, drained
110-g/3¾-oz. can smoked squid in oil (or just squid if you can't find smoked)
500 ml/2 cups chicken stock (made with 1 stock cube)
2 x 200-g/7-oz. cans chicken breast, drained, rinsed and cut into 2.5-cm/1-inch cubes
85-g/3-oz. can smoked mussels in oil
a few sprigs of fresh flat-leaf parsley, chopped
salt and freshly ground black pepper
lemon wedges, for squeezing

Serves 4

Fry the onion in half the olive oil in a large heavy-based frying pan/skillet for a few minutes until softened, then add the garlic, the chopped peppers, smoked paprika, turmeric and tomato purée/paste. Season generously with salt and black pepper and cook for a couple of minutes, stirring frequently. You'll have a thick red paste at this stage.

Stir in the rice, green beans and can of smoked squid (including the oil). Add the stock and bring to a simmer. Once it's bubbling, give it one final stir, then add the chicken, turn the heat to medium-low and simmer, covered with a tight-fitting lid, for 12 minutes.

Once cooked, remove the lid and scatter the smoked mussels (including their oil) and the remaining olive oil over the top, garnish with the strips of jarred peppers and continue cooking for a couple more minutes to help scorch the bottom of the rice a little.

Turn off the heat and leave to rest for a couple of minutes before serving. Season again with a pinch of salt, garnish with chopped parsley and serve with lemon wedges.

Gold
RICH AND CREAMY
COCONUT
MILK
KARYATIS
MIXED
HOT
CHILLIES
205g
MEDIUM
BIJOUX

STEWS & CURRIES

BLACK TARKA DHAL

This comforting dish uses canned black lentils to create a creamy dhal and then oil is infused with tempered spices to create a deliciously flavoursome tarka. You can create an homage to the yellow split pea (channa dhal) variation using a 220-g/8-oz. can of pease pudding mixed with 125 ml/½ cup hot water and 60 ml/¼ cup vegetable oil as the base and then follow the rest of this recipe for the tempered spices.

400-g/14-oz. can black beluga lentils, drained and rinsed
½ vegetable stock cube
a splash of vegetable oil
1 onion, diced
30 g/2 tablespoons butter or coconut oil, as preferred
1 teaspoon ground turmeric
1 tablespoon ground cumin
1 teaspoon cumin seeds
1 teaspoon fennel seeds
1 teaspoon garam masala
3 garlic cloves, chopped
5-cm/2-inch piece of fresh ginger, peeled and grated
6 tomatoes from a 400-g/14-oz. can cherry tomatoes
1 teaspoon salt
½ fresh green chilli/chile, chopped
12 curry leaves
a few sprigs of fresh coriander/cilantro, to serve
lime wedges, for squeezing

Serves 2 as a main; 4 as a side

Tip the rinsed black lentils into a heavy-based saucepan, add 100 ml/⅓ cup plus 1 tablespoon water and crumble in the ½ stock cube. Bring to a simmer and cook for a few minutes, stirring occasionally, until the lentils have a thick consistency.

In a separate pan, add a splash of oil and fry the onion for about 10–12 minutes over a medium heat until soft and caramelized. Once golden, lower the heat, add half the butter and stir in all the spices. When the butter foams, add the garlic, ginger, tomatoes, salt and chopped chilli/chile and leave on the heat for a few minutes to reduce any excess liquid in the pan (crush the tomatoes with the back of a fork). Once you have a thick consistency, pour the spice mixture into the dhal and stir vigorously until it starts bubbling, then remove from the heat.

In a clean plan, heat the remaining butter until it foams, then fry the curry leaves for a minute. Drizzle the burnt butter and curry leaves over the top of the dhal. Serve with a few torn sprigs of fresh coriander/cilantro and wedges of lime.

CHANA SAAG PANEER

Canned spinach makes quick work of my own recipe for this popular Indian curry, comprising chickpeas, spinach and paneer, especially as I always have a can or two conveniently stashed away in a kitchen cupboard. This is delicious on its own, but feel free to serve with warmed naan breads or plain basmati rice and topped with a dollop of mango chutney. I should also mention that any leftovers reheated and served with a poached egg on top work well for breakfast. I wish I could say that was just a rumour I'd heard…

380-g/13½-oz. can leaf spinach
250-g/9-oz. pack paneer cheese (or halloumi will work too)
1 tablespoon ground cumin
a splash of olive oil
1 teaspoon cumin seeds
1 teaspoon fennel seeds
2 onions, diced
½ teaspoon ground turmeric
1 tablespoon garam masala
2.5-cm/1-inch piece of fresh ginger, peeled and grated
4 garlic cloves, chopped
2 dried whole red chillies/chiles (or a pinch of chilli/hot red pepper flakes)
400-g/14-oz. can chickpeas, drained
1 tablespoon tomato purée/paste
1 teaspoon salt
½ x 400-g/14-oz. can coconut milk

TO SERVE
lime wedges, for squeezing
boiled rice or naan bread
mango chutney (optional)

Serves 2 as a main; 4 as a side

Start with the spinach – pour the contents of the can into a sieve/strainer and use the back of a spoon to push down on the spinach, extracting as much liquid as possible. Leave this sitting in the sieve/strainer over a bowl while you prepare the rest of the ingredients.

Cut the paneer cheese into 2.5-cm/1-inch cubes and dust with half the ground cumin. Heat a splash of oil in a frying pan/skillet over a high heat, add the paneer and fry for just a couple of minutes until golden, then remove from the pan.

Add a splash more oil to the pan along with the cumin and fennel seeds and sweat the diced onions for about 6 minutes until caramelized and golden. Add the remaining spices, ginger, garlic and chillies/chiles and cook for 30 seconds, then add the drained chickpeas and tomato purée/paste. Tip in the spinach with the salt and stir to incorporate it with the rest of the ingredients. Fold in half a can of coconut milk, warm through until it bubbles, stirring frequently, then remove from the heat.

Serve in comforting bowls to snuggle round with a wedge of lime and some boiled rice or a chunk of ripped naan for company; a swirl of the remaining coconut milk over the top is a nice touch.

BANANA BLOSSOM & COCONUT CURRY

Banana blossoms are fleshy, purple flowers which grow at the tip of banana clusters. Their chunky, flaky texture makes them an ideal substitute for fish. Available in supermarkets and online, they are a huge export of Goa, so I've adapted a Goan-style fish curry, replacing fish with banana blossoms to keep it vegan. If you don't have all the spices, use garam masala and curry powder.

1 large white onion, coarsely chopped
4 garlic cloves, peeled
5-cm/2-inch piece of fresh ginger, peeled and coarsely chopped
1 teaspoon salt
olive oil, for frying
½ teaspoon ground turmeric
1 tablespoon paprika
1 tablespoon demerara/turbinado sugar
½ x 400-g/14-oz. can cherry tomatoes, drained
a bunch of fresh coriander/cilantro, chopped
50 g/½ cup ground almonds
400-ml/14-oz. can coconut milk
2 tablespoons cider vinegar
2 x 400-g/14-oz. cans banana blossoms (also called banana heart)
100 g/¾ cup plain/all-purpose flour
freshly squeezed juice of ½ a lime
salt and freshly ground black pepper
boiled rice or flatbreads, to serve

MASALA SPICE MIX

1 tablespoon coriander seeds
1 tablespoon cumin seeds
1 star anise
2 cardamom pods
6 cloves
1 dried chilli/chile

Serves 4

In a large dry pan, toast all the masala spices for 30 seconds (take care not to burn them), then tip into a food processor with the onion, garlic, ginger, salt and a few tablespoons of water and blend to a paste. (Or grate the onion and use a pestle and mortar to grind the spices, if preferred.)

Add 45 ml/3 tablespoons of olive oil to the same pan and fry the blended mixture over a low heat for 15–20 minutes or until it turns a rich golden-brown colour. Stir in the turmeric, paprika, sugar, drained cherry tomatoes, most of the coriander/cilantro (save a few leaves to garnish) and ground almonds and pour in the coconut milk and vinegar. Simmer for 5 minutes or until the sauce has thickened slightly, then remove from the heat. Taste, adding more vinegar or sugar to get the balance of flavours right – it should be slightly tangy but balanced with the sweetness from the sugar.

While that's resting, drain the banana blossoms, rinse and pat dry with paper towels. Season with salt and pepper and dust in the flour, shaking off any excess flour. Heat a little olive oil in a griddle pan, add the banana blossoms and fry for a minute or two on each side until slightly charred.

Return the curry back to the heat and as soon as it starts to bubble, lay the banana blossoms on top, leave to warm through for a minute, then take to the table to serve straight from the pan. Garnish with the remaining fresh coriander/cilantro over the top, along with a squeeze of lime juice. Serve with rice or flatbreads.

RED JACKFRUIT CURRY

While spending time in Southeast Asia, I fell in love with the varied cuisines right across the region. My version of a red curry using canned ingredients is quick to make, and while it strays from anything remotely authentic, it features some of those headline flavours you'd expect from a Thai red curry. If you enjoy heat, include the whole chilli/chile in the paste, seeds and all; alternatively, just use the flesh for a slightly milder version. If you want it really hot, use a few small bird's eye chillies/chiles.

60 ml/4 tablespoons olive oil
2 x 410-g/14½-oz. cans jackfruit, drained and rinsed
400-g/14-oz. can coconut milk
1 tablespoon fish sauce
1 tablespoon brown sugar
1 lime
300-g/10½-oz. can marrowfat processed peas, drained and rinsed
a few fresh Thai basil leaves (optional)
boiled rice, to serve (optional)

RED CURRY PASTE

a handful of fresh coriander/cilantro
1 onion, coarsely chopped
4 garlic cloves, coarsely chopped
7.5-cm/3-inch piece of fresh ginger, peeled and coarsely chopped
2 fresh red chillies/chiles, coarsely chopped, plus 1 to garnish
2 lemongrass stalks (optional)
80 g/2¾ oz. roasted red (bell) peppers, from a jar or can
3 anchovy fillets from a can (optional)

Serves 4

To make the paste, roughly trim the stalks from the coriander/cilantro leaves. Set the leaves aside. Place the stalks in a food processor with all the paste ingredients and about 2 tablespoons water and blend to a paste. If you don't have a food processor, use a bowl and a hand blender, or use a hand grater to grate the onions and ginger and finely chop the rest.

Add the oil to a heavy-based pan set over a medium heat and pour in the red curry paste, stirring it into the oil. Reduce the heat to low and cook for about 10 minutes, stirring occasionally to stop it catching on the bottom of the pan. After 10 minutes, stir in the jackfruit, ensuring it's fully coated in the paste, then pour in the coconut milk, reserving a few tablespoons of the milk for later. Add the fish sauce, sugar and juice of half a lime plus about 4 tablespoons water. Leave the curry to simmer for about 8 minutes for the flavours to infuse and thicken slightly; if it gets too thick, add another splash of water.

Just before the end of cooking, fold the marrowfat processed peas into the curry along with the Thai basil leaves, if using. Finally, taste the curry, adding more fish sauce, sugar, lime juice or chilli/chile to suit your preference, then remove from the heat.

Garnish with a swirl of the leftover coconut milk, chopped coriander/cilantro leaves and sliced red chilli/chile.

LENTIL & ROASTED FRANKFURTER STEW

After working all day in a kitchen in France, I'd relax over a simple meal of saucisses aux lentilles vertes at a roadside café. This got me thinking... and then my Mum roasted frankfurters for my kids and I was surprised by how good they tasted with a crispy roasted skin! Et voila! This recipe was born.

400-g/14-oz. can frankfurters, drained
1 onion, diced
a splash of olive oil
3 garlic cloves, sliced
2 x 400-g/14-oz. cans green lentils, drained
2 tablespoons tomato purée/paste
150 ml/2⁄3 cup red wine
3 sprigs of fresh thyme
2 bay leaves
300-g/10½-oz. can sliced carrots, drained
1 chicken stock cube
1 teaspoon cider vinegar
a handful of freshly chopped flat-leaf parsley, to garnish
crusty bread, to serve

Serves 4

Preheat the oven to 180°C fan/200°C/400°F/Gas 6.

Score the frankfurters twice along the top at an angle, ensuring you don't cut all the way through. Place the frankfurters in a lightly oiled roasting pan and roast in the preheated oven for 25 minutes until the skin goes crisp.

Meanwhile, in a large frying pan/skillet, fry the diced onion in a splash of olive oil for a few minutes to soften, then add the garlic and cook for another minute. Add the drained lentils to the pan, along with the tomato purée/paste, red wine, thyme and bay leaves. Reduce over a high heat until the wine has almost fully evaporated, then add the drained carrots. Crumble in the stock cube along with 100 ml/1⁄3 cup plus 1 tablespoon hot water and cook on a low simmer until the sauce has reduced by half, then fold in the vinegar and remove from the heat.

Arrange the frankfurters on the lentils and garnish with a scattering of fresh parsley and a drizzle of olive oil, then serve from the pan/skillet with some crusty bread on the side.

SMOKY BLACK BEAN STEW WITH SWEET POTATOES & MINTED YOGURT DRESSING

This deliciously easy black bean stew is complemented by roasted sweet potato and a cooling yogurt and mint dressing. You can cook this either on the stovetop (as I did) or in a hot oven, covered, for 30 minutes. It's a very versatile recipe so feel free to swap sweet potatoes for any squash or root vegetable. I make this with a chicken stock cube for extra flavour, but a vegetarian stock cube works just fine if preferred. Serve with creamy mashed potatoes or rice.

750 g/1 lb. 10 oz. sweet potatoes
a splash of olive oil
1 tablespoon dried thyme
1 onion, diced
1 fresh red chilli/chile, deseeded and chopped
3 garlic cloves, crushed
1½ teaspoons ground cumin
1 teaspoon smoked paprika
1 teaspoon ground cinnamon
400-g/14-oz. can cherry tomatoes
2 x 400-g/14-oz. cans black beans, drained and rinsed
1 chicken or vegetable stock cube
a pinch of sugar
a few sprigs of fresh coriander/cilantro, chopped, to garnish
salt and freshly ground black pepper

MINTED YOGURT DRESSING

1 garlic clove
250 g/1 cup Greek yogurt
2 tablespoons freshly chopped mint or 2 teaspoons dried mint
1 tablespoon freshly squeezed lemon juice
1½ teaspoons ground cumin

Serves 4

Preheat the oven to 200°C fan/220°C/425°F/Gas 7.

Peel and cut the sweet potatoes into irregular wedges and place on a baking sheet. Drizzle with olive oil, then season with salt, pepper and dried thyme. Bake in the preheated oven for 20–30 minutes until cooked through and slightly charred, then remove and set aside until the black bean stew is ready.

For the minted yogurt dressing, crush the garlic clove and combine with the yogurt, mint, lemon juice, a generous pinch of salt and the cumin. Set aside.

In a large pan, fry the onion in another splash of olive oil for 5 minutes until soft, then stir through the chilli/chile and crushed garlic for a minute. Add the cumin, paprika and cinnamon, quickly followed by the tomatoes and black beans. Fill the used tomato can with cold water and pour into the pan, crumble in the stock cube and season with salt and pepper and a generous pinch of sugar. Part-cover the pan and simmer over a low heat for about 15 minutes or until the sauce has reduced and thickened. Fold the cooked sweet potatoes into the stew.

Taste for seasoning, scatter the coriander/cilantro over the top and add a swirl of the minted yogurt dressing, with the rest served on the side.

MEDITERRANEAN BEAN STEW WITH CHORIZO

Canned ratatouille is a great go-to store-cupboard ingredient as it adds aubergine/eggplant, peppers and courgettes/zucchini all in one go! Here I've combined it with cannellini beans and chorizo to make a smoky Mediterranean-style stew. Serve with plenty of crusty bread.

1 onion, thickly sliced
30 ml/2 tablespoons olive oil, plus extra to drizzle
2 garlic cloves, sliced
100 g/3½ oz. cooking chorizo, sliced
1 tablespoon tomato purée/paste
400-g/14-oz. can cannellini beans, drained and rinsed
400-g/14-oz. can borlotti/cranberry beans, drained and rinsed
2 x 400-g/14-oz. cans ratatouille
a pinch of chilli/hot red pepper flakes
a few sprigs of fresh flat-leaf parsley, chopped
sea salt flakes and freshly ground black pepper
crusty bread, to serve

Serves 4

Fry the onion in the olive oil in a large pan over a very high heat for 30 seconds – just long enough to char slightly. Turn the heat down, add the garlic and chorizo and leave to cook for a minute until the chorizo starts to release its oils, then add the tomato purée/paste and cook for another minute.

Now add all the remaining ingredients except the parsley. Bring to a simmer, then turn the heat to low, season generously with salt and pepper and leave to cook for 5 minutes. Finish with the chopped parsley scattered over the top and a decent drizzle of olive oil, and serve with chunks of crusty bread.

SMOKED OYSTER GUMBO

A gumbo is a slow-cooked thing of beauty, a blend of flavours and ingredients celebrating the melting pot of cultures that has contributed to its back story. I've fond memories of diving into a bowl of it in New Orleans many years ago and discovered then that the key to a good gumbo is the dark rich roux which gives it a unique silky consistency. My quicker interpretation of this classic features canned smoked oysters, which feel right for a dish originating from Louisiana, and also optional jumbo prawns/shrimp, which I add 5 minutes before the end of cooking.

400-g/14-oz. can okra, drained
4 tablespoons cider vinegar
60 ml/¼ cup vegetable oil
80 g/2¾ oz. ready-to-eat smoked sausage, cut into 1-cm/½-inch slices
40 g/generous ¼ cup plain/all-purpose flour
1 onion, diced
1 celery stick/stalk, diced
1 tablespoon ground cumin
1 tablespoon smoked paprika
a pinch of cayenne pepper
1 tablespoon dried mixed herbs
a pinch of sugar
1 tablespoon tomato purée/paste
½ x 400-g/14-oz. jar roasted red (bell) peppers, drained and chopped
3 garlic cloves, chopped
400 ml/1¾ cups chicken or vegetable stock (made with 1 stock cube)
12 frozen large prawns/jumbo shrimp, (optional)
½ teaspoon salt
2 x 85-g/3-oz. cans smoked oysters
a few sprigs of fresh flat-leaf parsley, chopped
olive oil, to drizzle
rustic bread, to serve

Serves 4

Drain and rinse the okra in a sieve/strainer, gently push down to release some of the excess liquid, then place in a bowl with 3 tablespoons of the vinegar and leave to steep.

Heat the oil in a large heavy-based saucepan and fry the sausage for a few minutes over a medium heat until golden, then remove with a slotted spoon, leaving the oil in the pan.

Add all the flour to the oil, mix thoroughly and leave to cook over a medium heat for a couple of minutes, then add the onion and celery and cook for 6–8 minutes or until the roux turns a deep golden colour. Now add all the spices, dried herbs and sugar and stir in the tomato purée/paste. Cook for a couple of minutes, then add the canned peppers and garlic and cook for a couple more minutes. Slowly pour in the chicken stock, stirring thoroughly as you do to avoid lumps. Add the frozen prawns/shrimp to the pan (if using), return the cooked sausage to the pan and simmer for a few minutes over a low heat, stirring occasionally.

Gently fold the drained okra into the pan. Bring it up to a gentle simmer, add the salt and turn the heat to low. Add more stock if it is too thick (it should be the consistency of double/heavy cream). Add the smoked oysters (and their oil) to the pan and gently fold in to avoid breaking them up. Taste, adding more salt, cayenne pepper or the remaining vinegar as needed. Garnish with parsley and a drizzle of olive oil. Serve in warm bowls with rustic bread on the side.

eat wholesome
FOOD CO.
ORGANIC
CHICK PE
High Protein & Fibr
Non-BPA
BUTTE
BEANS

OVEN BAKES

GREEK GIGANTES PLAKI

These giant baked beans in tomato sauce are a firm favourite throughout the Aegean. In my book Orexi! I included an indulgent recipe for this dish, slow-cooked dried beans, lazily simmering away over an entire afternoon, but these will be good to go within the hour! A great alternative if you are pushed for time. A nice touch is to crumble some feta cheese over the top just before serving – its tangy saltiness complements the sweet tomato sauce really well.

1 onion, diced
a splash of olive oil
2 garlic cloves, sliced
½ teaspoon ground cinnamon
½ tablespoon coriander seeds, crushed
1 teaspoon paprika
300-g/10½-oz. can sliced carrots, drained
1 tablespoon tomato purée/paste
400-g/14-oz. can cherry tomatoes
400-g/14-oz. can butter beans, drained
½ teaspoon sugar
a few sprigs of fresh flat-leaf parsley, chopped
salt and freshly ground black pepper

Serves 2 as main; 4 as a side

Preheat the oven to 160°C fan/180°C/350°F/Gas 4.

In a heavy-based, ovenproof frying pan/skillet, fry the onion in a splash of olive oil for 5 minutes until softened, then add the garlic and cook for another minute. Stir in the cinnamon, crushed coriander seeds and paprika followed by the carrots, and then mash with a potato masher – this is quite easy and quick. Add a splash more oil if needed but keep on the heat, and add the tomato purée/paste, can of cherry tomatoes including all the juices and the butter beans. Using the cherry tomato can, fill it halfway with water, swirl and pour that into the pan (this will be about 250 ml/1 cup water). Finally, season generously with salt, pepper and the sugar and place the whole pan into the preheated oven for 25 minutes.

Once done, remove the pan from the oven and leave to cool for a few minutes before serving. If it's too thick, add a little water to loosen. Serve hot or at room temperature, with a final drizzle of olive oil and freshly chopped parsley scattered over the top.

GNOCCHI, BLUE CHEESE & ASPARAGUS BAKE

Oven-baked gnocchi bathed in a creamy asparagus sauce and with pockets of melting blue cheese – sheer comfort-food heaven! Using creamy asparagus soup, canned asparagus and long-life gnocchi means you can create this delicious supper in no time at all with minimum effort. Win win.

425-g/15-oz. can or jar asparagus spears, drained
a splash of olive oil
1 onion, diced
2 garlic cloves, sliced
a knob/pat of butter
800 g/1 lb. 12 oz. long-life gnocchi
400-g/14-oz. can cream of asparagus soup
75 g/2¾ oz. blue cheese, such as Stilton or Shropshire blue
salt and freshly ground black pepper
rustic bread, to serve

Serves 4

Preheat the oven to 200°C fan/220°C/425°F/Gas 7.

Drain the asparagus, reserve a few spears to garnish, then chop the rest and set aside.

Add a splash of olive oil to a large ovenproof pan and fry the onion for a few minutes until soft, then stir through the garlic for 30 seconds. Add the chopped asparagus and season generously. Cook for a couple of minutes and while cooking, press down on the asparagus to break it down a little more, then remove the mixture from the pan to a plate.

Add the butter to the same pan (no need to wipe it first) and fry the uncooked gnocchi just long enough to colour – a couple of minutes should do it. Return the chopped asparagus and onion mixture to the pan and pour in the can of soup and a few tablespoons of water. Mix everything together, bring to a gentle simmer and remove from the heat.

Scatter over the reserved asparagus spears and crumble the blue cheese over the top. Place the whole pan in the preheated oven for 12 minutes. Serve straight from the pan with rustic bread to mop up the sauce.

CANNELLINI BEAN & ARTICHOKE GRATIN

I'm very lucky to work with some amazing people who are as passionate about food as I am. I've had many a long conversation with my editor, Julia Charles, discussing recipes and techniques. So I am delighted that Julia has allowed me to include her delicious cannellini bean and artichoke gratin recipe (she also said that if I didn't include it she'd make me sound unedjamacated...).

a splash of olive oil
a knob/pat of butter
1 large leek, halved lengthways, then finely sliced widthways
1 onion, finely sliced
1 garlic clove, crushed
400-g/14-oz. can artichoke hearts, drained and halved
400-g/14-oz. can cannellini beans, drained and rinsed
finely grated lemon zest and freshly squeezed juice, to taste
125 ml/½ cup white wine
a few sprigs of fresh thyme or a pinch of dried herbes de provence
300 ml/1¼ cups single/light cream
150 g/1½ cups grated/shredded any mild semi-hard cheese
salt and freshly ground black pepper

TO SERVE
rustic bread
a tomato and chive salad

Serves 4

Preheat the oven to 160°C fan/180°C/350°F/Gas 4.

Add a splash of olive oil and a knob/pat of butter to a heavy-based pan and sauté the leek and onion for 5–6 minutes until they soften, then stir through the garlic for a minute and remove from the heat. Decant the contents of the pan into a large mixing bowl along with the halved artichoke hearts and cannellini beans, season with salt, black pepper, a grating of lemon zest and a good squeeze of lemon juice. Set aside.

Give the pan a wipe and return to the heat; pour in the wine, add the thyme leaves and reduce by a quarter, just to burn off the alcohol. Remove from the heat and pour in the cream, stirring as you do. Return to the heat and bring back to a simmer for a few minutes to thicken the sauce slightly. Add the contents of the mixing bowl into the pan with the sauce, fold everything together, then pour into a shallow gratin dish (or leave in the pan if ovenproof) and scatter the cheese over the top.

Bake in the preheated oven for 20 minutes, remove and leave to rest for 5 minutes before serving.

Serve with rustic bread and a side dish of lightly dressed sliced ripe tomatoes and a scattering of chives.

PUNCHY CHILLI WITH CHIPOTLES IN ADOBO

Canned chipotle peppers in adobo sauce are smoky, hot and lip-smackingly good. You won't need a whole can for this recipe so transfer the leftovers to a sterilized jar, pour in a little olive oil to create a seal and store in the fridge where they'll last for ages. For the meat element here, I've used canned ox tongue rather than beef – yes, it's an unusual ingredient that has fallen out of fashion but give it a go! I've fried it until crisp and used it to top a spicy chilli sauce – I promise you'll be converted.

2 x 184-g/6½-oz. cans ox tongue
a splash of vegetable oil
a splash of olive oil
1 large onion, sliced
4 garlic cloves, finely chopped
1 tablespoon ground cumin
½ tablespoon smoked paprika
1 teaspoon ground cinnamon
1 tablespoon dried oregano
60 ml/4 tablespoons tomato purée/paste
200-g/7-oz. can chipotles in adobo sauce – you'll need 2 heaped tablespoons, chopped
400-g/14-oz. can red kidney beans, drained and rinsed
1 teaspoon runny honey
350 ml/1½ cups beef stock
½ tablespoon dark soy sauce
1 tablespoon gravy granules
salt and freshly ground black pepper

TO SERVE
a few slices of jalapeño
a few sprigs of fresh coriander/cilantro
boiled rice or tortilla chips
200 g/1 cup Greek yogurt
grated/shredded Cheddar cheese

Serves 4

Preheat the oven to 180°C fan/200°C/400°F/Gas 6.

Finely slice the ox tongue, then run a knife over the slices to break them down a little. Heat a heavy-based ovenproof pan until almost smoking, then fry the ox tongue in a splash of vegetable oil (you may need to do this in two batches). It will splutter and pop at first and then eventually start to foam after a few minutes over a high heat. Once it foams, continue cooking for another 5 minutes or until the foaming subsides and the slices are really crisp, then tip out of the pan onto a plate lined with paper towels and set aside.

Reduce the heat to medium. Give the pan a quick wipe if needed, add a splash of olive oil and fry the onion for about 5–10 minutes or until it softens and starts to caramelize. Once golden, stir through the garlic for a minute, then add all the spices, dried oregano, tomato purée/paste and chipotles in adobo sauce and stir thoroughly. Add the beans and honey and season generously with salt and black pepper. Pour in the beef stock and soy sauce along with the gravy granules, and bring the pan to a simmer, stirring as you do. Once bubbling, remove from the heat, scatter the fried ox tongue over the top, give the pan a little shake and place in the preheated oven for 12 minutes.

Garnish with sliced jalapeños and coriander/cilantro leaves and serve with boiled rice or tortilla chips, Greek yogurt and grated cheese.

CHICKEN & MUSHROOM LASAGNE BAKE

My friend Victoria, who makes the most incredible sourdough, introduced me to canned chicken in white sauce, so I owe the inspiration of this recipe to her. This simple layered pasta bake makes use of good-quality canned chicken and mushrooms for a quick yet incredibly tasty family meal. You can swap the mushrooms for pretty much any other canned vegetable you like. If you want to cheat even more (which I'm all for) you can use store-bought white sauce for the topping and just add grated cheese. Serve with a simple green leaf salad dressed with olive oil and red wine vinegar.

2 x 400-g/14-oz. cans chunky chicken in white sauce
2 x 290-g/10-oz. cans sliced mushrooms, drained
500 ml/2 cups milk
30 g/2 tablespoons butter
30 g/3⅔ tablespoons plain/all-purpose flour
a pinch of freshly grated nutmeg
1 tablespoon olive oil
9 sheets dried lasagne pasta
120 g/scant 1⅓ cups grated/shredded Cheddar cheese
salt and freshly ground black pepper

Serves 4

Preheat the oven to 160°C fan/180°C/350°F/Gas 4.

In a large bowl mix together the cans of chicken in white sauce and the drained mushrooms. Swirl around the chicken cans using 100 ml/⅓ cup of the milk, to get the last dregs of the sauce, and pour into the bowl. Mix everything together and season generously with salt and freshly ground black pepper and set aside.

To make the white sauce, put the butter and flour into a small pan over a low heat. Stir as the butter melts, to form a roux and cook for a minute. Remove from the heat and whisk in the remaining milk, a little at a time. Grate a little nutmeg into the pan, season with salt and pepper and return to the heat, whisking all the while. When it starts to bubble, remove from the heat and stir in half the cheese, then set aside.

Drizzle the olive oil over the base of a 30 x 20-cm/12 x 8-inch baking dish. Lay three lasagne sheets down, pour over half the chicken and mushroom mixture, then do another layer of lasagne and a layer of chicken. Place a third layer of lasagne sheets over the chicken mixture and top with the white sauce. Scatter over the remaining cheese and bake in the preheated oven for 45 minutes. Leave to rest for 10 minutes before serving with a green salad, if you wish.

CHICKEN KIEV WITH BABY HASSELBACK POTATOES

This is my student life summed up in a single meal! I loved a chicken kiev, especially served with marrowfat processed peas which I'm still partial to. This recipe is a great example of a full meal created using store-cupboard ingredients.

1 fat garlic clove, crushed
a few sprigs of fresh flat-leaf parsley, finely chopped
50 g/3½ tablespoons salted butter, at room temperature
567-g/20-oz. can new potatoes, drained
200-g/7-oz. can chicken breast
2 scant tablespoons plain/all-purpose flour, plus extra for dusting
1 egg
50 g/1 cup breadcrumbs (about 2 slices of bread)
1 tablespoon vegetable oil
300-g/10½-oz. can marrowfat processed peas
a pinch of dried mint or leaves from 2 sprigs of fresh mint, chopped
salt and freshly ground black pepper

Serves 2

Preheat the oven to 200°C fan/220°C/425°F/Gas 7.

Mix the garlic and parsley with half the butter. Quickly roll the garlic butter into two balls and place in the freezer. (If the butter is too soft to roll, pop it in the fridge for 5 minutes.)

Thinly slice the potatoes three-quarters of the way through – be careful not to cut them all the way. Place on a baking sheet, cut side up, melt the remaining butter and brush liberally over the potatoes. Season and bake for 40 minutes.

Meanwhile, empty the chicken into a bowl and mash with the back of a fork. Season with black pepper, sprinkle over the flour and mix it through the chicken. Whisk the egg in a separate bowl and pour half onto the chicken. Mash it altogether. Divide the chicken mixture in two, form a rough ball with your hands and push a frozen garlic butter ball into the centre. Massage the chicken around the butter in a slight oval shape (try to keep the butter in the middle of the chicken). Repeat with the second portion of chicken.

In a bowl, mix the breadcrumbs with the vegetable oil. Carefully roll each kiev in flour, then in the remaining egg, then in the breadcrumbs to coat. Place on a baking sheet and bake alongside the potatoes for 20 minutes. The potatoes and chicken kievs should be ready at about the same time, when the kievs are golden and crisp and the potatoes are roasted with a tinge of colour and have opened up slightly.

Tip the peas into a pan, bring to the boil, then simmer to reduce the liquid to a double/heavy cream consistency. Remove from the heat and stir in the mint before serving.

CHICKEN & DILL MEATBALLS ON LEMONY ORZO

Meatballs are always crowd-pleasing family fare. Here I make meatballs from canned chicken and dill and bake them in the oven, along with garden peas as it makes them a little crispy and adds texture to the dish. Served with orzo pasta, flavoured with lemon, this is light and perfect for summer.

200-g/7-oz. can chicken breast
1 tablespoon freshly chopped dill, plus a few sprigs to garnish
1 egg, whisked
olive oil
300-g/10½-oz. can garden peas, drained and rinsed
1 onion, diced
2 garlic cloves, sliced
250 g/9 oz. dried orzo (rice-sized pasta shapes)
1 chicken stock cube
freshly grated zest and juice of 1 lemon
60 g/¼ cup Greek yogurt
a pinch of chilli/hot red pepper flakes (optional)
salt and freshly ground black pepper

Serves 4

Preheat the oven to 200°C fan/220°C/425°F/Gas 7.

Empty the can of chicken breast into a bowl and gently mash with the back of a fork, then season with a pinch of salt, freshly ground black pepper and the dill. Mix in the whisked egg, roll the mixture into ping-pong ball-sized meatballs (you should get around 12 meatballs). Place on a baking sheet and drizzle over a little olive oil. Shake any excess water off the rinsed peas and scatter them over the baking tray with the meatballs. Bake in the preheated oven for about 18 minutes.

Meanwhile, fry the onion in a little olive oil in a deep pan for about 5 minutes until soft, then stir through the garlic and orzo for 30 seconds. Crumble in the stock cube and fill the pan with enough hot water for the level to be at least 2.5 cm/1 inch above the orzo. Cook according to the packet instructions (usually 8–10 minutes, depending on the brand) and top up with more hot water if needed while cooking. Drain the pan when the orzo is cooked.

When the chicken balls are done, tip the orzo mixture onto the baking sheet. Add the lemon juice and the yogurt and mix together, taking care not to break up the meatballs. Pop back in the oven for 5 minutes to warm through. Garnish with the remaining dill, lemon zest, a pinch of chilli/hot red pepper flakes and a little drizzle of olive oil.

CHICKEN & MUSHROOM PIE

This recipe uses canned chicken for ultimate convenience, coupled with an additional cheat of using chicken soup for an instant creamy sauce. You can't go wrong – cook the filling in the pan, top it with pastry and whack it in the oven. It's ready to serve the whole family 20 minutes later!

2 x 200-g/7-oz. cans chicken breast
50 g/6 tablespoons plain/all-purpose flour, for dusting
285-g/10-oz. can whole button mushrooms, drained
a splash of olive oil
1 onion, diced
1 garlic clove, chopped
leaves from 2 sprigs of fresh thyme
2 bay leaves
400-g/14-oz. can cream of chicken soup
200 g/7 oz. ready-made puff pastry
1 egg
a splash of milk
salt and freshly ground black pepper
canned baby carrots and petit pois, to serve
a knob/pat of butter, to serve
gravy, to serve (optional)

Serves 4

Preheat the oven to 200°C fan/220°C/425°F/Gas 7.

Dice the chicken breast into 2.5-cm/1-inch cubes and dust in a little flour, then set aside. Drain the mushrooms in a sieve/strainer, pushing them down to release any excess moisture, then dust in flour.

Add a splash of olive oil to an ovenproof pan and fry the chicken and mushrooms for a few minutes until the chicken has browned a little (you may need to do this in batches if it starts to overcrowd the pan). Remove both from the pan and set aside. Add another splash of olive oil if needed and fry the onion for a few minutes until softened, then stir through the garlic for 30 seconds. Return the chicken and mushrooms to the pan, add the thyme and bay leaves and pour in three-quarters of the chicken soup. Simmer for a few minutes until the filling thickens, adding a splash more soup if it gets too thick. Season generously with salt and pepper and remove the pan from the heat.

On a lightly flour-dusted work surface roll out the pastry 2.5–5 cm/1–2 inches larger than the top of the ovenproof pan, and about 5 mm/¼ inch thick. Drape the pastry over the top of the filling, tucking the edges of the pastry inside the pan. Prick a few times with a fork and feel free to add any cute pastry cut-outs on top as decoration.

Whisk the egg with a splash of milk and brush over the top of the pastry, sprinkle with salt and bake in the preheated oven for 18–20 minutes or until the pastry is golden and cooked. Serve with canned petit pois and carrots with a knob/pat of butter, and lots of instant gravy – I love that stuff.

POTATO-STUFFED CHEESY PEPPERS

These Romano peppers with a canned potato stuffing are so quick to make and are utterly delicious. They work perfectly as a light meal served with salad or they make a wonderful accompaniment to a more substantial meal. If your peppers are quite large, pop them in the oven first for 10 minutes to start the cooking process.

4 Romano peppers
300-g/10½-oz. can new potatoes
100 g/½ cup Greek yogurt
1 garlic clove, crushed
100 g/1 cup Cheddar cheese, grated/shredded
50 g/⅔ cup Parmesan cheese, grated
30 g/½ cup fresh breadcrumbs
2 tablespoons freshly chopped chives
1½ teaspoons olive oil
salt and freshly ground black pepper

Serves 2 as a main; 4 as a side

Preheat the oven to 200°C fan/220°C/425°F/Gas 7.

Halve the Romano peppers lengthways straight through the stalk, removing any pith and seeds from inside, and place all eight halves cut side up on a baking sheet.

Drain the potatoes, place in a bowl and mash as thoroughly as possible – the smoother the better. Fold the yogurt, garlic, all the Cheddar cheese and half the Parmesan cheese into the potatoes, then season generously with black pepper and a pinch of salt. Divide the mixture between the peppers, spooning it inside each one.

For the topping, mix the breadcrumbs with the remaining Parmesan, the chives and olive oil and scatter evenly over the stuffed pepper halves.

Bake in the preheated oven for 20 minutes or until the tops are crisp and golden. Serve with a green salad.

HEART OF PALM TARTINE

This recipe is quite simple to make, and the punchy chutney base works so well with the topping of creamy hearts of palm. I like to use a spicy red onion chutney, but any type of onion chutney will work. The topping of breadcrumbs is intended to be very simple, but if you fancy it you can dot pieces of goat's cheese or cream cheese over the top as well.

375 g/13 oz. ready-made puff pastry
½ x 220-g/8-oz. jar red onion chutney
2 x 410-g/14½-oz. cans hearts of palm, drained and sliced into 1-cm/½-inch discs
30 g/2 tablespoons butter, melted
2 tablespoons fresh breadcrumbs
salt and freshly ground black pepper

Serves 4

Preheat the oven to 200°C fan/220°C/425°F/Gas 7.

Roll out the pastry to fit a 30 x 20-cm/12 x 8-inch baking sheet and score a border 2.5-cm/1-inch in from the outer edges of the pastry. Bake uncovered in the preheated oven for 10 minutes. Remove from the oven, allow to cool for a few minutes, then press down the centre.

Spread the red onion chutney over the pastry base, then top with the heart of palm discs. Brush with melted butter, season with freshly ground black pepper and a pinch of salt and finish with a scattering of breadcrumbs over the top.

Return to the oven and bake for a further 10 minutes. This goes well with a light mixed leaf green salad.

HARVEST PIE

My harvest pie is packed with canned lentils and vegetables and uses potato and leek soup to bring everything together for a hearty and savoury supper. If you were feeling exceptionally lazy (as I must confess I am occasionally...), you can mix the filling directly in the pastry case and just top with a pastry lid, then into the oven for an even quicker fix.

500 g/1 lb. 2 oz. ready-made puff pastry
1 egg, whisked
2 x 400-g/14-oz. cans green lentils, drained and rinsed
400-g/14-oz can baby carrots and petit pois, drained and rinsed
400-g/14-oz can green beans, drained and rinsed
400-g/14-oz can potato and leek soup
25 g/3 tablespoons plain/all-purpose flour, plus extra for dusting
15 g/1 tablespoon butter, diced
1 teaspoon dried mixed herbs
1 teaspoon salt
½ teaspoon freshly ground black pepper
½ teaspoon curry powder

Serves 4

Preheat the oven to 200°C fan/220°C/425°F/Gas 7.

Cut the block of pastry in half and roll out one half on a floured work surface to about 3 mm/⅛ inch thick. Use this to line a 28 x 20-cm/11 x 8-inch baking pan, allowing the pastry to overhang the top lip of the pan. Line with baking parchment and baking beans (or raw rice, etc.) and blind bake in the preheated oven for 20 minutes. Remove from the oven, remove the parchment and baking beans, then brush with some of the whisked egg and return to the oven for another 5 minutes.

In a mixing bowl, gently fold all the remaining ingredients together. Pour into the baking pan on top of the cooked pastry and level out with the back of a spoon. Roll out the remaining pastry to cover the top, crimping around the edges to seal.

Pierce the top with a sharp knife to help the steam release, brush with the remaining egg and season the top. Bake in the oven for a further 30 minutes or until the top is golden. Leave to rest for at least 15 minutes to allow the filling to set before serving.

SALMON 'NDUJA WELLINGTON

This salmon and spinach wellington laced with spicy 'nduja (spreadable pork sausage) makes a stunning meal. 'Nduja is a useful ingredient as it keeps for ages in the fridge and goes with everything. Well, just about... I'm a big fan.

380-g/13½-oz. can leaf spinach, drained
1 onion, diced
1 tablespoon olive oil
3 garlic cloves, chopped
a small knob/pat of butter
300 g/10½ oz. ready-made puff pastry
plain/all-purpose flour, for dusting
60 ml/4 tablespoons 'nduja (or use a jar of 'nduja pesto or sundried tomato pesto)
1 tablespoon dried oregano
60 ml/4 tablespoons tomato purée/paste
2 x 213-g/7½-oz. cans pink salmon, drained, skin and bones removed
1 egg, whisked

TO SERVE
300-g/10½-oz. can broad/fava beans
400-g/14-oz. can baby carrots and petit pois
a knob/pat of butter
2 sprigs of fresh mint
hollandaise sauce or gravy
salt and freshly ground black pepper

Serves 4

Preheat the oven to 200°C fan/220°C/425°F/Gas 7.

Place the spinach in a sieve/strainer, pushing it down with the back of a spoon to squeeze out as much liquid as possible.

Fry the onion in the olive oil for a few minutes to soften and caramelize, then add the garlic and cook for another minute. Add the spinach and fry for a few more minutes until all the moisture has evaporated. Remove from the heat and fold in the butter, then spread the spinach onto a plate to cool down.

Roll out the pastry on a work surface dusted with flour to approximately 45 x 20 cm/18 x 8 inches and place on a piece of baking parchment. Mix the 'nduja, oregano and tomato purée/paste together and spread over the pastry with the back of a spoon, leaving a border of 2.5 cm/1 inch at the two short ends of the pastry. Spread the spinach over the top of the tomato mixture using the back of a fork to even it out.

Taking a small handful of salmon at a time, give it a very gentle squeeze to remove a little of the moisture and form a line of salmon the length of the pastry on one side (leave a gap of 2.5 cm/1 inch at both ends). Lift the parchment and roll the pastry over the salmon filling to make a tightly enclosed log. Pinch the ends together to seal and brush with egg. Make a few small slits in the top to let steam escape and season with a pinch of salt. Slide onto a large baking sheet. Bake in the preheated oven for 20–25 minutes or until golden.

Tip both cans of vegetables into a pan, heat until piping hot, then drain, stir through the butter and season well. Just before serving, garnish with mint leaves. Use a bread knife to carve the salmon wellington. Some say you should serve it with hollandaise sauce, but I love instant gravy with this one.

EST.1891
Epicure
ACK CHERRIES
440g
FOOD THOUGHTS
100%
BEST FOR BAKING
DELICIOUS &
NUTRITIOUS
SOIL ASSOCIATION
ORGANIC
SOLID PACK

SWEET TREATS

PEACH-APRICOT-PLUM CRUMBLE

I'm a great fan of adaptable recipes that allow me to make something on the spot without digging around for specific ingredients. This crumble can be put together in a flash, with whatever canned fruit you have, but I enjoy this combination in particular. The slight sharpness of the plums contrasts nicely with the sweetness of the peaches and apricots. In the colder months, steeping a little bag of mulled wine spices in the plum syrup adds lovely aromas and warming spice. Serve with canned custard or vanilla ice cream.

411-g/14½-oz. can peach slices
411-g/14½-oz. can apricot halves
567-g/20-oz. can plums
80 g/scant ½ cup demerara/turbinado sugar
1 tablespoon cornflour/cornstarch
1 teaspoon vanilla extract
a few drops of freshly squeezed lemon juice
200 g/1½ cups plain/all-purpose flour
100 g/7 tablespoons butter
30 g/⅓ cup rolled/porridge oats
400-g/14-oz. can custard/custard sauce or vanilla ice cream, to serve

28 x 20-cm/11 x 8-inch high-sided baking pan

Serves 6

Preheat the oven to 200°C fan/220°C/425°F/Gas 7.

Drain the peaches and apricots and put the fruit into the baking pan. Drain the plums, saving 150 ml/⅔ cup of the syrup in a bowl. If using plums that contain their stone/pit, use your hands to tear the plums in half to remove these and drop the flesh into the baking pan with the rest of the fruit. Add just over half the sugar and mix together.

Add the cornflour/cornstarch, vanilla extract and lemon juice to the bowl containing the reserved plum syrup; whisk together to combine (don't worry if you have a few small lumps of cornflour/cornstarch) and pour over the fruit.

In a large mixing bowl add the flour, remaining sugar and butter and work together with your fingertips to create a crumble mixture. Once fully combined, fold through the oats and scatter the mixture over the top of the fruit.

Bake in the preheated oven for 30 minutes, then let it rest for 5 minutes before serving with custard or ice cream.

PRUNES IN COFFEE SYRUP
WITH GREEK YOGURT & WALNUTS

This recipe can top and tail your day, satisfying the need for a morning caffeine fix or an after-dinner pick-me-up. The espresso adds a subtle bitterness to the prunes which offsets their natural caramel sweetness and toasted walnuts add a welcome crunch.

290-g/10-oz. can prunes in natural juice (you can use pitted or unpitted)
45 ml/1½ oz. freshly made espresso coffee (basically 1 shot)
2 teaspoons caster/granulated sugar
Greek yogurt, to serve (allow approx. 150 g/¾ cup per serving)
a small handful of toasted walnut halves, crushed, to serve

Serves 4

Decant the prune juice from the can into a small saucepan (you'll get about 200 ml/¾ cup) and pour in the shot of espresso and the sugar. Simmer over a medium heat until it starts to bubble, then drop in the prunes and continue to simmer until the juice is reduced by about half.

Leave to cool before spooning over Greek yogurt. Top with a few crushed walnuts for crunch.

SWEET 'DONUT' ARANCINI

These indulgent little arancini could be the love-child of a deep-fried doughnut and a can of rice pudding. They are light and creamy with the little surprise of sticky jam/jelly in the centre. They are very moreish – you have been warned!

400-g/14-oz can good-quality rice pudding/creamed rice
100 g/¾ cup self-raising/rising flour, plus 130 g/1 cup for dusting
2 eggs, whisked
100 g/2 cups fresh breadcrumbs (about 2–3 slices of read, grated)
500 ml/2 cups vegetable oil (enough for deep frying)
½ teaspoon ground cinnamon, plus extra for dusting
3 teaspoons strawberry jam/jelly
2 tablespoons icing/confectioners' sugar

Makes 6

When you open the can of rice pudding, most of the contents will have settled to the bottom. Discard the milky sauce on top, then tip the remaining rice pudding into a sieve/strainer.

Place three small bowls in a row: the first containing the flour for dusting, the second containing the whisked eggs and the third containing the breadcrumbs. Pour the oil for deep frying into a large heavy-based saucepan and begin to heat.

Tip the drained rice pudding into a mixing bowl. Gently fold in two-thirds of the remaining flour and all the cinnamon. Continue adding more flour until the mixture starts to hold together; it will be fairly loose – you're not making a dough.

Dust your hands with flour, take a heaped dessertspoonful of the rice pudding mixture and drop it into the small bowl of flour (to help it stop sticking to your hands); remove the spoonful of pudding mixture and gently form it into a ball by rolling between your palms, then poke your finger into the middle, about halfway in and fill with about ½ teaspoon jam/jelly, then pinch the top together to close the hole. Drop the ball back into the bowl of flour and roll around, then into the egg wash, then finally into the breadcrumbs to coat.

Test the oil temperature by dropping in some breadcrumbs; they should sizzle immediately but take 30 seconds to turn golden. Carefully lower the rice ball in and deep fry for a few minutes until golden. Remove using a slotted spoon and drain on paper towels while you finish the rest. Mix the remaining cinnamon with the icing/confectioners' sugar and dust over the top of the arancini. Serve warm.

BALSAMIC CHERRY TARTE TATIN

This sultry-looking tarte tatin recipe uses the syrup from the canned cherries with a splash of good-quality balsamic vinegar. It helps to cut through the sweetness of the reduced syrup and adds a little bite. Serve with whipped cream or vanilla ice cream on the side.

425-g/15-oz can cherries in syrup
50 g/¼ cup caster/granulated sugar
50 g/3½ tablespoons butter
1 vanilla pod/bean
1 teaspoon balsamic vinegar
200 g/7 oz. ready-made puff pastry
whipped cream or vanilla ice cream, to serve

28-cm/11-inch ovenproof frying pan/skillet

Serves 8

Preheat the oven to 200°C fan/220°C/425°F/Gas 7.

Drain the cherries in a sieve/strainer set over a bowl, then pour the syrup (about 500 ml/2 cups) into the ovenproof frying pan/skillet. Reduce the syrup over a gentle heat for about 8 minutes until thick, but keep a close eye on it to avoid burning! Remove from the heat, then stir in the sugar and butter. Split the vanilla pod/bean, scraping the seeds into the pan and dropping the pod/bean in as well, then return to the heat and simmer over a low heat, stirring occasionally, until the caramel pulls away from the edges and leaves gaps in the pan for a second when stirring (about another 3 minutes of cooking).

Once the cherry caramel looks like a loose jam, turn off the heat and fold in the cherries and balsamic vinegar. Roll out the pastry 2.5 cm/1 inch wider than your pan/skillet and lay over the top, tucking the edges into the pan. Poke a few holes in the top to help release the steam while cooking.

Bake in the preheated oven for 15 minutes or until the pastry has puffed up and turned golden. Remove from the oven and leave to cool for 5 minutes before running a knife around the edge to detach the pastry from the sides of the pan/skillet. Invert a plate over the top and in one swift movement, holding the plate in place, flip the whole thing over and carefully shuffle the pan from the top, revealing the tarte tatin. Serve with whipped cream or vanilla ice cream.

PUMPKIN & ALMOND CAKE

We're big fans of cakes and desserts in our household and having a standby can of pumpkin purée in the cupboard is perfect for creating this sweet treat at short notice. I use ground almonds in the cake to keep it moist and you really do need to leave it to cool until fully set. And it tastes even better the day after it's been baked, so cover it loosely with foil and enjoy any leftovers the next day. The next day? Ha! We've never actually seen it the 'next day'...

220 g/1 cup caster/granulated sugar
150 g/⅔ cup butter, at room temperature
4 eggs, whisked
175 g/1⅓ cups plain/all-purpose flour
1 tablespoon ground cinnamon
1 teaspoon ground cloves
1 teaspoon vanilla extract
425-g/15-oz. can unsweetened/natural pumpkin purée
100 g/1 cup ground almonds

20-cm/8-inch round cake pan, lined with parchment paper

Serves 8

Preheat the oven to 180°C fan/200°C/400°F/Gas 6.

Cream the sugar and butter together in a bowl, then add the whisked eggs and flour along with the spices and vanilla extract, mixing until smooth. Briefly whisk in the pumpkin purée, then mix in the ground almonds.

Once fully combined, pour the cake mixture into the parchment-lined cake pan and bake in the preheated oven for 1 hour. Leave to cool in the pan on a wire rack before serving.

CHAI-SPICED RHUBARB
WITH CREAMY COCONUT RICE

Indulgently creamy coconut rice made with arborio rice to maintain some chewiness and texture, topped with my 5-minute chai-spiced canned rhubarb makes for a delicious treat all year round. The rhubarb compote also works very well stirred into creamy Greek yogurt as a breakfast pot.

150 g/¾ cup arborio rice
500 ml/2 cups semi-skimmed/low-fat milk
60 g/¼ cup demerara/turbinado sugar
400-ml/14-oz. can coconut milk
50 g/⅔ cup flaked/chipped or desiccated/dried shredded coconut

CHAI-SPICED RHUBARB
540-g/19-oz. can rhubarb in syrup
5-cm/2-inch cinnamon stick
a pinch of ground allspice
a few grates of nutmeg
4 cardamom pods
3 cloves
50 g/¼ cup caster/granulated sugar
a pinch of salt
a slice of fresh ginger, 3 mm/⅛ inch thick

Serves 4

Start with the chai-spiced rhubarb. Pass the canned rhubarb through a sieve/strainer set over a small saucepan – you should end up with about 250 ml/1 cup rhubarb syrup in the pan. Put the rhubarb flesh into a shallow bowl and set aside.

Add all the spices, sugar, salt and ginger to the saucepan, bring to a simmer, stirring occasionally, and then reduce by about a third; it will darken and thicken slightly. Once reduced, pour the syrup through a sieve/strainer (to capture the spices) into the bowl with the rhubarb and leave it to steep until required.

For the rice pudding, pour the rice, milk, 1 tablespoon of the sugar and 300 ml/1¼ cups of the coconut milk into a saucepan and bring to a gentle simmer. Partially cover the pan and cook over a low heat for about 45 minutes or until the rice is tender, stirring occasionally to stop it catching on the bottom of the pan – you may have to add a splash more milk as you go. While that's cooking, toast the coconut in a dry frying pan/skillet until golden (it only takes a minute), then decant onto a plate to cool.

When the rice is cooked, remove from the heat and stir in the remaining sugar and coconut milk. Serve immediately, spooning some of the spiced rhubarb over each portion and scattering over a little of the toasted coconut.

BLACK BEAN BROWNIES

These moist and crumbly gluten-free brownies are completely delicious and you'd never know they were made with black beans! A food processor isn't essential here but it certainly helps. Once baked, leave to cool completely before removing from the baking pan and cutting.

400-g/14-oz can black beans, drained (if not making in a food processor, mash these with a fork until as smooth as possible)
a pinch of salt
1 teaspoon vanilla extract
80 ml/⅓ cup vegetable/flavourless oil
3 eggs
30 g/⅓ cup unsweetened cocoa powder, plus extra for dusting
60 g/⅔ cup porridge/rolled oats
100 g/½ cup soft brown sugar
1 tablespoon runny honey
40 g/¼ cup any chocolate chips
25 g/1 oz. hazelnuts, chopped

15 x 20-cm/6 x 8-inch baking pan, lined with parchment paper

a food processor (optional)

Makes about 12

Preheat the oven to 180°C fan/200°C/400°F/Gas 6.

Blend together the black beans, pinch of salt, vanilla extract and vegetable oil in the food processor until smooth. Crack the eggs into the puréed black bean mixture and pulse a couple of times to combine. Add the cocoa, oats, sugar and honey to the mixture and pulse again until combined. Fold in the chocolate chips and hazelnuts and pour the mixture into the lined baking pan. Bake in the preheated oven for 18 minutes.

Remove from the oven and leave to cool thoroughly in the pan. Dust with extra cocoa powder, then remove from the pan and cut into 12 pieces to serve.

INDEX

INDEX (CONTINUED)

ACKNOWLEDGEMENTS

This book is the result of a group of hugely talented people working together collectively towards a single goal, and me.

I owe my first debt of gratitude to my wife Anna, not only for her unwavering support but also for turning a blind eye to the bombsite that I turn our kitchen into for months on end. For smiling through gritted teeth as I present the SAME plate of food for the third time in a row with such minor alterations no one will notice except me. Anna, thank you darling.

My kids, thank you, not so much for helping me with the book, but for maintaining an element of bedlam that makes our weird lives and chaos in the kitchen feel like the norm. Eva, Lex, Luca – I love you all, even when you're acting like teenagers, years before your teenage years arrive.

Cindy Richards, my publisher, I am forever grateful for that meeting all those years ago that led you to welcoming me into the Ryland, Peters & Small author family and for believing in me. Thank you, I can't imagine doing this without you.

Julia Charles, my editor, who fluctuates seamlessly between being a friend and sanity checker and, with the skills of an encryption expert, manages to decipher my ramblings and turn them into eloquent sentences. She was joined this time in the ongoing battle with punctuation by Gillian Haslam, who kept my recipes coherent and was a joy to work with, even while telling me off, which is a skill in itself.

These beautiful pages wouldn't exist without the work of art director Leslie Harrington, food stylist Kathy Kordalis (who recreates every recipe with a flair I envy), prop stylist Polly Webb-Wilson, and photographer Mowie Kay, whose talent behind the camera knows no bounds (plus he makes me look good – cheque is in the post!).

In summary, thank you to you, my dream team; none of this would be possible without you. Theo x